Death at Dozier School

The Attempted Assassination of an American City

Dale Cox

2014

ISBN: 978-0692346334

Old Kitchen Books
Bascom, Florida 32423

Be ye all of one mind, having compassion one of another,
love as brethren, be pitiful, be courteous.
1 Peter 3:8

Contents

Introduction

THIS IS A BOOK ABOUT A CEMETERY. I clarify this now because the former Dozier School for Boys in Florida is surrounded by a whirlwind of allegations, claims, opinions, and in some cases, outright falsehoods. Many of these have been exacerbated by media coverage generated and often coordinated by employees of the University of South Florida (USF), an institution of higher learning in Tampa. The university has used more than half a million dollars in taxpayer funding to search for and exhume graves on the campus of the former institution for juvenile offenders. To quote one of the graduate students involved in the project, it was done in the name of "social justice."

Unfortunately, the Dozier School Cemetery is no better understood by the public at large today than it was before two years of research by USF and an accompanying frenzy of media coverage. The university has grown increasingly secretive about is work on the campus and on at least one occasion even went so far as to deny that it had released new information even as it provided a major report of findings to the State of Florida. Researchers once conducted media tours on the Dozier School campus and even allowed CNN unprecedented live access as the first graves were exhumed. Today they carefully hold their press conferences hundreds of miles away from the site and release only a trickle of information to a media that remains fixated on the fading narrative that the cemetery was a place where bodies were dumped following hundreds of "murders" and "abuse-related deaths" on the campus.

Why the dramatic change? This book will provide you with an opportunity to answer that question for yourself.

So then, this is a book about a cemetery. It is a history of the Dozier School or "Boot Hill" cemetery in Marianna, Florida. The goal is to make public the facts about the cemetery from its first interments more than 100 years ago to the present controversy that led to its destruction. This is not a book about the allegations of abuse that have been made against the school and its employees by groups of former students except where those allegations involve the cemetery or other rumored gravesites on campus. Much has been written about the "White House" – a structure on campus where corporal punishment was administered to students that has become a focal point of abuse allegations – but the building was not used for punishment purposes during most of the cemetery's active history. Only one burial is known to have taken place in the Dozier School Cemetery after the former ice cream factory now called the "White House" was converted for use as a storage and punishment facility. For reasons that will be explained in the book, the individual buried in that grave was not connected to the "White House" allegations.

On the pages that follow you will find a documented history of the cemetery and its use to bury unfortunate students and employees of the school for roughly fifty years. The story it presents is tragic. In some cases it is heart-breaking. Yet there are also moments of inspiration and heroism associated with some of the graves. Those stories are related as well, in hopes that the reader will gain a better appreciation for the noble actions of some residents of the school, students and employees alike.

I am deeply indebted to many individuals for their assistance in making this book possible. Some have requested that their names be kept anonymous and I have complied with their wishes. They know who they are and my sincere thanks are extended to them. My special appreciation is also due to Rose Davis, now retired, of the Florida Department of Law Enforcement (FDLE); Sue Tindel and Robert Earl Standland of the office of Jackson County Clerk of Courts Dale Guthrie; Matt Fuqua, Attorney at Law; Chief Hayes Baggett of the Marianna Police Department; Pat Crisp of the Chipola Historical Trust; Cindy Sloan, genealogist; Robert Daffin; Ruth Kinsolving; Danny Pate, former Superintendent of Dozier School for Boys; Sheriff Lou Roberts of Jackson County; Kay Tidwell Nichols; Rhonda Dykes of The Vintage Depot; Max Basford; Royce Reagan of Chipola College; former State Representative Marti Coley; Jeannie Pappas; Coy Goodson; the staff of the Florida State Archives and anyone not listed here that assisted in any way.

My appreciation is also due to Roger Dean Kiser, author of *The White House Boys: An American Tragedy*, for discussing his memories of life at Dozier School, the abuse allegations that surround the school and the activities of the organizations formed by former students. He has been kind and courteous and I have gained much from our discussions.

Thank you also to Gerard Solis and Lori Mohn of the Office of General Counsel at the University of South Florida (USF) for the courtesy and responsiveness they have shown in handling my numerous requests for information and documents under Florida's Sunshine Law and Public Records statutes.

Finally, my thanks are due to Dr. Mary Glowacki, State Archaeologist of Florida, and Ms. Julia C. Byrd, Florida Public Archaeology Network, for their kindness in meeting with me to discuss the Dozier School Cemetery exhumations, for listening to my concerns and for answering my many questions over the duration of the project.

As always, I am grateful to my sons – William Cox and Alan Cox – for listening to my thoughts and discussing the Dozier School controversy with me. Savannah Brininstool did a great job in helping with the editing of this volume. Thanks also to my mother, Pearl Cox, for reading the final draft.

May God bless and keep you all and shower his mercy and kindness upon you.

Dale Cox
November 30, 2014

For the women and men of the Florida Department of Law Enforcement.

Death at Dozier School

The Attempted Assassination of an American City

One

The Dozier School Cemetery

DOZIER SCHOL FOR BOYS, originally known as the State Reform School, was a facility for juvenile offenders that operated in Marianna, Florida, from 1900-2011. During the course of that long history, a number of students and employees of the school died from a variety of causes. Many were buried in the school cemetery, which is known locally and by former students and staff members alike as "Boot Hill."

Recent news coverage to the contrary, such cemeteries are not unusual at reform schools and prisons throughout the country. The "Chicken Hill" cemetery at the Kentucky State Reformatory, for example, has 96 recorded graves. The Boys Training School Cemetery in Missouri has at least 44 graves. The Bennie Lee Hill Memorial Cemetery at the former Kansas Boys Industrial School has twelve. The Illinois Girls School Cemetery has around 50, most of them infants born to girls sentenced to the school. Unmarked or unknown graves are not uncommon.[1]

Even in Florida the Dozier School Cemetery is small and far from unusual when compared to similar burial places at other state facilities dating from the same era. The State Prison Cemetery in Starke, for example, contains the graves of inmates and possibly others who died at Union Correctional Institution at Raiford and Florida State Prison in Starke. As of 1984, 629 people had been buried there. The Florida State Hospital in Chattahoochee has five known cemeteries where thousands of burials have taken place. Unmarked graves from its years as a state penitentiary have been found during construction projects.[2]

1

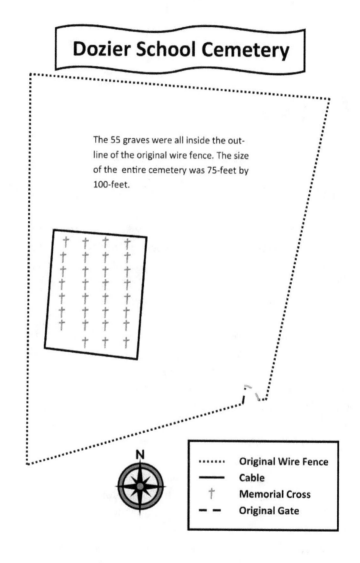

Dozier School Cemetery

The 55 graves were all inside the outline of the original wire fence. The size of the entire cemetery was 75-feet by 100-feet.

N

....	Original Wire Fence
——	Cable
†	Memorial Cross
– –	Original Gate

As similar as it might be to cemeteries at other institutions of its type across the country, the Dozier School Cemetery is different because it attracted the attention of six distinct groups or organizations: 1) former students who claim that other students were murdered by employees of the school, 2) Dr. Erin Kimmerle and fellow researchers at the University of South Florida (USF), 3) the office of Florida Attorney General Pam Bondi, 4) the office of U.S. Senator Bill Nelson, 5) the NAACP, and 5) the media. Supported in one way or another by all of these, the University of South Florida launched a project to dig up the graves in the cemetery – with or without the permission of any surviving next of kin of those known to be buried there.

USF's science project at Dozier School Cemetery will be discussed in greater detail in Chapter Nine. The research team believed as it went into the project that it would find two cemeteries, one on the South or "white" campus for white students and the known or "Boot Hill" cemetery on the North or "black" campus for black students. Former employees of the school and local residents with knowledge of its history denied that there were two cemeteries and maintained that the graves at "Boot Hill" contained all of those buried on campus, black and white.

In November 2012 and again in April 2013 the author announced on behalf of a small group of researchers that a thorough search of available state records and other documentation had confirmed the presence of 53 graves in the cemetery. USF released its "Documentation of the Boot Hill Cemetery" interim report in December 2012 concluding that there were 49 probable or possible grave shafts. The school's estimate was based on the results of a ground penetrating radar survey of the cemetery. The conclusions of the local research team were announced one month before USF's report was made public.[3]

The cemetery then consisted of a clearing in a wooded area with a small memorial area containing 31 crosses. Employees of the school who were present when the crosses were placed in the early 1990s indicated they were grouped as a memorial and were never intended to mark individual graves. The crosses were made with metal pipe and replaced 28 deteriorating concrete crosses that had been placed in a similar grouping on part of the cemetery during the 1960s. The number was expanded from 28 to 31 to reflect the number of burials indicated by the surviving school ledgers as well as two dogs and a peacock – pets of students – known to have been buried in the cemetery.[4]

Those familiar with the placement of the metal crosses in the 1990s as well as the original concrete crosses during the 1960s emphasized in interviews with the author that the small area of crosses was never thought to be the entire cemetery. Two eyewitnesses that saw the graves prior to the placement of the original memorial crosses recalled that the cemetery site was a somewhat overgrown area surrounded by a rusty wire fence. This was undoubtedly the fence shown on the USGS Cottondale-East Quadrangle Map published in 1952. It surrounded an area of roughly 100-feet by 50-feet and was constructed with its longest sides in an approximate north-south orientation.[5]

A former student recalled that he had been part of a crew assigned to maintain the cemetery during the 1950s. He remembered it as a grassy area surrounded by a wire fence and gate. His description matches that of the other two eyewitnesses and also confirms that the actual cemetery was surrounded by a wire fence that enclosed a much larger area than the cable that surrounded the memorial crosses prior to the exhumation of the graves in 2013. This is an important observation as it confirms that the dimensions of the cemetery as shown on the USGS topographic map were much larger than those of the small enclosure that surrounded the metal crosses.[6]

The location of the cemetery was never "secret" as claimed in some media reports but instead was well-known on campus and in the community. In fact, the isolated little graveyard attracted the attention of the school's chaplain during the 1960s. His daughter recalled in 2014 that her father – Archie McDaniel, Jr. – was greatly moved by the existence of the graves and sought to convince state authorities to appropriate money for the enhancement and care of the cemetery. Failing in that effort he obtained the permission of administrators for the school's Boy Scouts to better mark the graves. The daughter remembers walking up the hill to the cemetery with her father prior to the beginning of the project and seeing little more than a few deteriorating wooden crosses at the site.[7]

The presence of wooden grave markers in the cemetery is confirmed by the school's former maintenance supervisor, Coy Goodson. He assisted with the Boy Scouts project and also remembered seeing a few wooden crosses marking graves, but recalled that they were badly deteriorated. Goodson and the other members of the maintenance staff helped make the concrete crosses that the Scouts placed in the cemetery during the 1960s. He recalled that depressions could be seen indicating the presence of other graves on the hilltop but that it was impossible to determine exactly where most of the burials had taken place. Since the Boy Scouts and employees helping them were unable to identify and mark all of the individual graves, they decided instead to cluster the concrete crosses in a memorial area marking the cemetery site in general.[8]

The confirmation of the various eyewitnesses that a few deteriorating wooden crosses could be seen at the site prior to the construction of the memorial is significant. The cemetery has been widely described by the media as "unmarked" and USF has used the term "clandestine" to describe the graves. If the graves were originally marked by wooden crosses, however, they were neither "unmarked" nor "clandestine." Under Florida law, there is a significant difference between marked and unmarked graves.

The bigger questions, of course, surrounded the graves themselves. How many people were buried in the cemetery? Was there a second cemetery as asserted by USF and some former students? Were there hidden graves in other places on campus? Did the graves contain the bodies of students murdered by staff members? Would the bones of those buried in the cemetery prove allegations by former students of brutal beatings at the school?

These questions figured prominently in news coverage as the media demanded that USF be allowed to dig up the graves at Dozier School. Most of the answers, however, were available before the first shovel full of dirt was turned.

According to an October 1906 article written for the Marianna *Times-Courier* by Frank McDonald, the first death at what was then the State Reform School took place during its first six years of operation:

The inmates are rosy-cheeked and robust, and their health is and has been excellent. There have been but two deaths since the institution was started, and of these one came to the school with organic disease of the heart, while the other was recaptured escape, who succumbed, notwithstanding the best of care and medical attention, from the inroads of long exposure at an inclement season.[9]

The identities of the two students were not included in McDonald's article although he did note that the population at the school then consisted of 39 boys and 4 girls. In the six years that had passed since its opening 171 juveniles had been received there and 128 discharged. Several of those discharged were escapees that were recaptured and then sent on to other correctional facilities.[10]

The earliest records of the school were destroyed when the dormitory that also contained the superintendent's office was destroyed by fire in 1914, so nothing else is known at this time about the two student deaths mentioned by McDonald. It is not known whether they were buried at the school or returned home for burial.[11]

USF researchers evidently did not locate this article while preparing their interim report for the Florida Division of Historical Resources. Believing that all information regarding deaths and potential burials at the school should be of significance to a team researching deaths and potential burials at the school, I sent the article quoted above to Gerard Solis, the Assistant General Counsel for USF.

He has been cordial in his communications with me and informed me by email on September 24, 2013, that he had forwarded my email to Dr. Kimmerle. To date neither the professor nor any member of her team has attempted to contact me or has sought permission to review documentation about the cemetery in my possession.

The next known death at the State Reform School also took place during its first ten years of operation. Superintendent Burrell T. Morgan passed away in 1910:

Marianna, Fla., June 3. – (Special.) – Supt. B.T. Morgan, of the state reform school here, died at the institution today, after an illness of three weeks with heart and stomach troubles. He was thought to be recovering until this morning when he suffered a relapse and within a few hours died.

His mother and two brothers survive him. Mr. Morgan had been superintendent of the reform school for the past seventeen months and was held in the highest esteem by his associates and the inmates.

The funeral will occur tomorrow afternoon. [12]

The superintendent's death was also overlooked by the research team from the University of South Florida. He was buried at Marianna's Riverside Cemetery on June 4, 1910. Born on July 8, 1862, he was 47 years old at the time of his death. [13]

The next known deaths at the school took place four years later. It is possible that future research in newspaper archives and private collections might reveal that there were additional deaths from 1900-1914. For the present, however the deaths of Superintendent Morgan and the two students during those years are the only known deaths at the school not also confirmed by official documentation.

---

[1] Various cemetery surveys available through USGenWeb sites.

[2] *Ibid.*

[3] "Chipola Talks" program, Chipola College TV, November 2012; *Tampa Bay Times*, April 2014; Kimmerle EH, Estabrook R, Wells EC, Jackson AT. 2012. Documentation of the Boot Hill Cemetery (8JA1860) at the former Arthur G. Dozier School for Boys, Interim Report, Division of Historical Resources, Permit No. 1112.032, December 10, 2012.

[4] Wendy Johnson, "Boot Hill", Northwest Florida Magazine, 1989; Personal Communication, Danny Pate, 2013.

[5] Personal Communication, Coy Goodson, 2013; Personal Communication, Jeannie Pappas, 2014; USGS Quadrangle Map for Cottondale-East, 1952.

[6] Former Student #1, statement made in online posting, 2013.

[7] Personal Communication, Jeannie Pappas, 2014.

[8] Personal Communication, Coy Goodson, 2013.

[9] McDonald, Frank, "History and Progress of State Reform School," Marianna *Times-Courier*, October 1906, reprinted in *The Pensacola Journal*, October 24, 1906, p. 4.

[10] *Ibid.*

[11] "Ten Lives Lost when Florida Reform School Burns at Marianna," *Tampa Tribune*, November 19, 1914, p. 1.

[12] *Montgomery Advertiser*, June 4, 1910.

[13] Don Brock and Treadwell Sims, "Survey of Riverside Cemetery," July 14 & 15, 1956. Manuscript in private collection of the author.

Two

The 1914 Fire

THE YEAR 1914 WAS A MOMENTOUS ONE IN HITORY. An estimated 1,047 people died when the RMS *Empress of Ireland* went down after colliding with another vessel in the St. Lawrence River. The RMS *Titanic* had carried 1,500 to the bottom just two years earlier. Central America witnessed the passage of the first vessel passed through the now famous Panama Canal in 1914 while in Sarajevo a Serbian nationalist assassinated Archduke Franz Ferdinand of Austria and sparked World War I. An attempt to assassinate the brutal Rasputin failed in 1914. Babe Ruth played in his first professional baseball game that year. Charlie Chaplin appeared in the first feature-length silent film. Ford Motor Company introduced the 8-hour work day and the Federal Reserve Bank opened for business. And in Marianna an unexplained series of fires continued to take place on the campus of the Florida Reform School.

These fires took place with alarming frequency over the first 14 years of the school's operation. One in February 1906 had killed six mules and three horses, while also destroying corn, hay and 32 barrels of syrup. The cause was arson and the suggestion was raised that former guards had been responsible. "It is supposed that the barn was set on fire to spite the superintendent," reported the *Pensacola Journal*, "as several guards of been discharged for various reasons." Tracking dogs brought to the scene, however, failed to detect the trail of the perpetrator.[1]

The fires continued over the next five years with growing frequency and on January 25, 1911, a new brick barn burned to the ground with almost disastrous consequences:

That the school's loss is not greater is miraculous, as the dormitory for colored inmates is within fifty to seventy-five feet of the barn. None of the livestock or farming implements were lost. This will badly cripple the school as all of the supplies of this kind [i.e. hay and cattle feed] were in this one barn.[2]

The outbreak of a fire described as "spectacular and fierce" so close to one of the school's two dormitories alarmed employees, authorities and reporters alike. Damage was estimated at $10,000, a massive figure in that day and age, with 1,000 bales of hay and several tons of cattle feet being destroyed, along with a supposedly "fireproof" barn.[3]

Newspaper clippings indicate additional fires took place over the next three years, although none resulted in destruction on the scale of the 1911 blaze. All were blamed on an "incendiary" or arsonist[4]

The escalating series of fires came to a dramatic end in the predawn darkness of November 18, 1914:

W.H. Bell, acting superintendent, has just wired from Marianna that main building white school was destroyed by fire last night, and eight boys and two officers dead. Please call meeting of Board of Managers with least possible delay. Have matter exhaustively investigated and let me have report.[5]

Immediate reports from the scene indicated that the fire had been discovered by a night watchman at around 3:30 a.m. The watchman passed the main dormitory and saw no problems at 3:15 a.m., but when he returned from his rounds fifteen minutes later, a large fire was burning on the ground floor near the base of the main stairway. He began to call out to the boys and employees sleeping on the second and third floors of the building, trying to alert them to the danger.[6]

The calls of the watchman alerted Severino Gustinez, a student considered so trustworthy by administrators that he had been given employment at the school and assigned to watch over the younger boys who were housed on the second floor of the east wing of the dormitory. Although some media reports of the time claimed that fire drills had never been held at the school, the opposite appears to have been true.[7]

Realizing the danger, Gustinez called out "Fire Drill!" to awaken the young students under his charge. Sleepily they arose from their beds and immediately formed into the proper lines for evacuating the building. Realizing that he could not take them down the main stairway due to the fire, he led them to the west end of their wing and down the stairway to safety. Thanks to "Toto," all of the younger students made it out of the building without incident.[8]

Leaving the small boys in charge of a guard named Register, Gustinez went back into the building where he found an older boy nicknamed "Monkey Wrench" lost in the smoke. Carrying "Monkey Wrench" in his arms, he made his way back to the stairway but found the door now in flames. Risking his own body to bring "Monkey Wrench" to safety, Gustinez leaped through the burning doorway. Both survived, although the heroic rescuer suffered slight injuries.[9]

Another older student named Walter Tucker made it out, but was unable to find his bunk mate Button Shaw. Desperate to save his friend, he went back into the burning building, found Shaw still in bed, pulled him out and carried him up to the third floor of the building. The tower that rose above the center of the structure had windows that also functioned as skylights. Dragging Shaw up into the tower and through one of these windows, Tucker carried him across the roof and down the fire escape to safety.[10]

The acting superintendent of the school – later claims to the contrary aside – was in the building and asleep on the third floor when the fire broke out. Making his way up to the tower, W.H. Bell helped most of the older boys escape through a window and then down the fire escape to the ground.[11]

Having already saved many lives, Bell now joined a desperate effort to save two employees and a student who could be seen trapped inside a locked grate that blocked access to the fire escape from the second floor:

...The office being in flames, he procured an axe and with the assistance of Mr. Allen, one of the guards, he climbed to the landing of the fire escape at the second floor, where three men were trying to make their escape. He succeeded

in breaking the locks of the barred grating to the window, but was unable to get the metal frame out of the window. In the meantime, the floors gave way and the inmates were hurried to their doom.[12]

Two of the men who died as Bell and Allen tried to save them were Bennett Evans, the school carpenter, and Charles M. Evans, his son who was employed as a guard. Charles had made it out of the building, but was unable to find his father and went back inside to save him. He found Bennett looking for him in the smoke and tried to bring him and a student they found lost in the smoke to safety, but found their escape barred by the locked grate. All were killed when the floor collapsed beneath them.[13]

Despite folklore repeated second hand by Dr. Erin Kimmerle and other researchers from the University of South Florida, there was no mention of any kind in the eyewitness accounts of the fire, let alone any actual evidence, that any of the students who died in the 1914 fire were chained to their bunks. In fact, eyewitness account indicates that all who died were moving freely inside the building and could have escaped.

The *Tampa Tribune*, for example, reported that most of the dead were in the west wing of the building farther from the fire than the smaller boys who were led to safety by Severino Gustinez. They became "panic-stricken" the newspaper reported, and lost their lives as a result.[14]

According to the *Tribune*, the guard named Register went back into the building after helping secure the smaller boys in a safe place. He found a group of older boys still inside and led them to a stairway by which escape was still possible. Frightened by the smoke that filled the stairwell, however, they panicked and went back deeper into the building to the locked fire escape. They lost their lives as a result.

Within thirty minutes of the time the fire was discovered, the "white dormitory" of the Florida Industrial School for Boys burned to the ground. By the time the sun rose over the horrible scene, only the ruined sections of walls could still be seen.

Shock spread across Jackson County and then Florida as citizens learned of the deadly fire. Initial reports indicated that 10 people had died, 8 students and 2 employees. The Pensacola Journal, Tampa Tribune, Miami Herald,

Montgomery Advertiser, Atlanta Constitution and dozens of other newspapers identified them as follows:

Bennett Evans, Employee
Charles Evans, Employee
Joe Wethersbee, Student
Walter Fisher, Student
Clarence Parrott, Student
Louis Fernandez, Student
Harry Wells, Student
Earl E. Morris, Student
Clifford Jefford, Student
Waldo Drew, Student

Two other names – S. Barnett and Louis Haffin - also surfaced briefly in association with the fire. The name of Haffin appeared in the Pensacola Journal's initial coverage of the fire and was picked up by Idaho Statesman. The name Barnett is shown only in the initial report of the coroner's inquest held in Jackson County on the day after the fire. The evidence indicates, however, that neither Barnett nor Haffin were actual victims of the fire. The Pensacola newspaper corrected its initial report with a note that there had been some confusion about the identities of those killed. The name of "S. Barnett" was removed from the paper's list of the dead. County officials soon clarified their own list of the dead by eliminating the name "Louis Haffin." The final report of the county grand jury lists the ten names given above.

Such mistakes are common in the hours after a major disaster, as the media demonstrated with its wild claims of widespread murders at the Louisiana Super Dome following Hurricane Katrina when in fact there were none. Both the media and local officials quickly corrected their errors, but this did not stop employees of the University of South Florida (USF) from inflating their death totals at the school by maintaining in their interim report that Barnett and Haffin really died in the fire.

With the corrections that took place in the two days following the fire, the final list of dead consisted of ten names. Other problems with the count, however, quickly became apparent.

While the bodies recovered were in extremely poor condition, there simply were not enough of them to account for 10 deaths, let along the 12 claimed by modern USF employees. The Tampa Tribune, for example, reported on November 20, 1914, that the body of Waldo Drew, a student from St. Petersburg missing since the fire, could not be found. His mother, Mrs. L.C. Drew, had been notified by telegram that her son had died, only to learn from media reports that he could not be found.

There was speculation that Drew's body might have been entirely incinerated, but this appeared unlikely as at least parts of other bodies were found. Officials of the school subsequently concluded that he had likely taken advantage of the chaos to escape. The school had no security fence and the two night watchmen were busy with Superintendent Bell in trying to save the lives of other students.

Nor was Drew alone in remaining unaccounted for after the fire. A second boy, Earl E. Morris, also was found to be missing. His name appeared on the original lists of the dead and, as was the case with Drew, it was assumed his body had been completely incinerated. The mystery regarding Drew was never solved, but Morris resurfaced in Georgia after the fire where newspaper reports indicate he was arrested by law enforcement officers. The discovery of Morris still alive and in Georgia after the fire removed his name from the list of the dead.

The final tally, including Waldo Drew who may or may not have died in the blaze, is as follows:

Bennett Evans, Employee
Charles Evans, Employee
Joe Wethersbee, Student
Walter Fisher, Student
Clarence Parrott, Student
Louis Fernandez, Student
Harry Wells, Student
Clifford Jefford, Student
Waldo Drew, Student (May have escaped)

According to telegrams sent by Superintendent Bell to next of kin, the bodies were buried at the school. Long-standing tradition in Jackson County indicates they were interred on the hilltop now dubbed "Boot Hill." This was confirmed by the USF exhumation project which uncovered charred human remains buried in coffins at the cemetery.

Although initial media reports blamed an oil lamp for starting the fire, evidence quickly grew that the blaze had been intentionally set. In view of the large number of arson fires that had taken place on the campus in the 14 years since the school opened, this was a logical direction for the investigation. The coroner's jury ruled the fire as an arson, but its report was completed very early in the investigation. Law enforcement officers, however, agreed and quickly developed information that a man named H.H. Caldwell had threatened to "blow up" the school.

Caldwell had come to the Florida Industrial School in the days before the fire to demand the release of his son, 16-year-old George W. Caldwell. When he was told that the school could not release the student without a court order, Caldwell allegedly became irate and warned that he would blow up the school unless his son was released. He quickly emerged as a suspect in the fire investigation.

USF employees misidentified the man in their interim report as "George W. Coldwell" of Laurel Hill, Florida. (Note: George W. Caldwell's name was misspelled as "Coldwell" on the 1920 census). George W. Caldwell of Laurel Hill, Florida, however, was only 16 years old at the time of the fire, having been born in Alabama in 1898. USF's claim aside, it seems highly unlikely that 16 year old would have had a son old enough to be at the school in 1914. In fact, George Caldwell was a student at the school when the fire took place and it was his father, H.H. Caldwell, who became a suspect in the investigation.

Based largely on circumstantial evidence – primarily the allegations of eyewitnesses that he had threatened to "blow up" the school – authorities from Jackson County arrested H.H. Caldwell on November 20, 1914, and lodged him in the Jackson County Jail. The grand jury, however, determined that there was no direct evidence linking him to the fire and returned a "no true bill" in his case. He was released from jail.

Researchers from the University of South Florida have made questionable claims (since revised) that as many as twelve people died in the fire. Initial reports from the scene, however, placed the number at ten (two employees and eight students). Subsequent investigation revealed that the actual number was somewhat lower.

The official state investigation of the fire that destroyed the "white" dormitory and administrative offices of the State Reform School on November 18, 1914, took five months to complete. With Attorney General Thomas F. West leading the probe, the members of Florida's Board of Institutions heard from dozens of witnesses and examined forensic evidence from the scene of the blaze. They also visited the scene of the fire and viewed the ruins for themselves.

The board filed its final report with Governor Park Trammell on April 21, 1915. The members concluded, as had the Jackson County Coroner's Jury, that the fire was intentionally set:

Two inmates who were sent to the barn a few hours before the fire occurred, testified to seeing a man, whom they claim to have recognized, run from the barn. Another inmate, who was aroused by the return of these two, remarked that he could see a man near the bakery, and was told by the first two who the man was.[15]

The intruder seen near the barn was H.H. Caldwell, who was mentioned above. The report went on to detail what happened inside the dormitory when the fire was discovered:

...An employee went to the lower floor, passing within ten feet of where the fire originated; returning to his room he went again to bed, but before going to sleep "heard a roaring," and on opening his door discovered the fire under considerable headway, near the foot of the east stairway. He gave the alarm, the night watchman promptly unlocked all dormitories and ordered the boys into fire drill formation, taking charge of those from one dormitory.[16]

The "night watchman" mentioned in the report was Severino Gustinez, the trusted older student who had been made a Trustee and assigned to watch over the safety of the boys in the dormitory after hours. As was noted earlier, he led the younger boys to safety while Acting Superintendent W.H. Bell and others took the older students from their wing up through the tower and across the roof to safety. In this way, the board members reported, 95 students were saved.[17]

Three students died when they refused to follow Bell out through the smoke after he told them to wrap their coats around their heads and follow him. A fourth student, described in the report as "somewhat mentally deficient," was carried out to safety but became disoriented and ran back into the building. He also died.[18]

A fifth student, the investigation concluded, died while trying to save the life of Acting Superintendent Bell:

One young hero lost his life in an attempt to rescue the acting superintendent, whom it was thought had not been awakened, but who had gained safety by going over the roof. Two employees, father and son, were lost after gaining safety, each going back into the building seeking the other.[19]

The final death toll from the fire, according to the official report, was seven. This number is three less than originally reported by the media of the time and five less than the University of South Florida (USF) claimed in its interim report released prior to the beginning of its project to dig up the Dozier School Cemetery. The Board of Institutions, led by the Attorney General of Florida, concluded that two employees and five students lost their lives in the blaze.[20]

Of the eight students originally reported as having been killed in the fire, it is known that Earl E. Morris took advantage of the confusion to escape. It is also known, based on written reports of the time, that the body of Waldo Drew was never found. His disappearance remains a mystery to this day. The identity of the third student that the Board learned had not died in the fire was not disclosed.

The Board of Institutions also addressed the issue of the locked fire escape doors:

...It being necessary to keep the inmates in confinement at night, the fire escapes were locked, the keys being in the office on the main floor in a place known to all about the building. However, had these fire escapes been opened and that method of escape adopted, it is the testimony of those present that the rapidity of progress of the fire would have increased, rather than decreased, the casualty loss.[21]

In its interim report released last year, the University of South Florida quoted another study which claimed that some of the dead had been held on shackles on the third floor of the dorm and were unable to escape. That earlier study, however, was based on folklore. Not one single original document or media report included such a claim.[22]

It appears most likely that the folk tale – as such stories often do – confused two fires that took place at about the same time in history. Several inmates of a convict camp run by the Aycock Brothers Lumber Company died when the stockade in which they were housed caught fire on October 7, 1905. Those inmates were unable to escape because of the shackles that chained them to their bunks.

The privately-run camp was located near the Jackson and Washington County line. It is probable that the individual who repeated the folk tale about inmates being burned to death while shackled to their bunks was remembering stories of the Aycock fire and not the one at the State Reform School.

Media reports from 1914 indicate that some students from the destroyed dormitory shared the dorm for African-American students after the fire, while others were provided shelter by local families until new housing could be built. The state decided against housing so many students in a single building again and converted the school to a cottage system. This led to fewer boys living in each structure with married couples employed to serve as "parents" over each cottage.

Was the fire an arson or was it the result of a tragic accident? The answer to that question may never be known. Different investigations reached different conclusions on the matter.

In the final analysis, it appears that 8 or possibly 9 people (2 employees and 6 or 7 students) died in the tragic fire that destroyed the "white dormitory" on November 18, 1914, although the Board of Managers lowered this number to seven. These fatalities raised the total number of known deaths at the school in 1900-1914 to 10-13. Two students and one employee died there in 1900-1910 and another unidentified student died in 1911. The fire also destroyed the administrative offices of the school and all the records kept there.

---

[1] "Fire at State Reform School," report from Marianna dated February 28, 1906, *Pensacola Journal*, March 1, 1906, p. 1.
[2] *Pensacola News*, January 1911, clipping in Singletary Collection.

[3] *Ibid.*

[4] Clippings from the Marianna *Times-Courier*, 1911-1914, Singletary Collection.

[5] Gov. Park Trammell to Hon. W.H. Milton, President of the Board of Governors, November 18, 1914, Singletary Collection.

[6] "Heroic Tampa Boy saves many lives at Marianna Fire," datelined Marianna, November 20, 1914, *Tampa Tribune*, November 21, 1914, p. 1.

[7] *Ibid.*

[8] *Ibid.*

[9] *Ibid.*

[10] *Ibid.*

[11] Anonymous, "Ten Lives Lost When Florida Reform School Burns at Marianna," November 18, 1914, report reprinted in numerous newspapers across the United States.

[12] *Ibid.*

[13] *Ibid.*

[14] "Heroic Tampa Boy saves many lives at Marianna Fire," datelines Marianna, November 20, 1914, *Tampa Tribune*, November 21, 1914, p. 1.

[15] Report of the State Board of Institutions to Gov. Park Trammell, April 21, 1915.

[16] *Ibid.*

[17] *Ibid.*

[18] *Ibid.*

[19] *Ibid.*

[20] *Ibid.*

[21] *Ibid.*

[22] USF, Interim Report, pp. 77-84.

PHOTO 1 ACTUAL DORMITORY DESTROYED BY FIRE ON NOVEMBER 18, 1914.

PHOTO 2 STRUCTURE USF CLAIMED WAS IDENTICAL TO DORMITORY.

PHOTO 3 ACTUAL STRUCTURE IDENTICAL TO BURNED DORM.

PHOTO 4 BOOT HILL (IN BACKGROUND) DURING THE 1930S.

Three

1918 Spanish Influenza

THE REFORM SCHOOL BECAME KNOWN AS THE FLORIDA INDUSTRIAL SCHOOL FOR BOYS during the year of the fatal 1914 fire. The loss of the "white" dormitory created a dramatic housing shortage on the campus but there is no indication that judges across the state held back on sentencing additional juveniles to the facility. The student population, in fact, grew dramatically over the next few years.

The school's more than 100 white students were temporarily crowded into the surviving dormitory already occupied by African American students. Contrary to an assertion by the University of South Florida, however, this situation was not endured for more than a few days. Local residents stepped forward to help students and administrators in the crisis by offering to house boys in their homes until new facilities could be constructed. This gesture on the part of the community quickly relieved the overcrowding of the "black" dormitory and provided safe quarters for students as construction went forward on the new South Campus cottages.

Three deaths were reported at the Florida Industrial School for Boys in the year after the fire. Scott Martin, Granville Rogers and Willie Fisher died in 1915 but their burial locations are not known.

Three more deaths at the school took place in 1916, all students from the North or "Colored" campus. Records identify them as Sim Williams, 18, who died on February 28, 1916; Tillman Mohind, 17, who died on May 25, 1916, and James Joshua, age unknown, who died on an unspecified day that same year. No causes of death were reported for the three students, but their deaths were noted in school reports.[1]

No deaths were reported for 1917, even though the United States glimpsed the first manifestations of the Spanish Influenza that fall. The virulent strain targeted the young with a viciousness seldom experienced and America's death rate rose during the fourth quarter of 1917. The rise, however, was minimal to what the world would experience the following year.

The next recorded death at the school was that of Thomas Aikins, a 12-year-old African American student. He died on April 16, 1918. No cause of death was listed. A 13-year-old white student, Lee Gaalsby, died on October 6, 1918. While the cause of his death was not listed in official records, school administrators did note that he was an escapee. A third student, 6-year-old George Grissam, was actually paroled to the care of a local family when he developed chronic gastritis. He died on October 23, 1918.[2]

It should be noted that administrators at the school had inspired the editorial ire of Tampa newspapers four years earlier when they refused to accept three 6 and 7 year old children delivered to their doors by authorities from Hillsborough County. Senator William Hall Milton, president of the school's board of managers, wrote to Governor Park Trammell that the Florida Industrial School for Boys "was never intended as a nursery." He and the other members of the board instructed the superintendent not to accept children who were too young or in ill-health. The Tampa media exploded in fury.[3]

"3 PICKANINNIES HAVE NO EXISTENCE IN LAW" blared a headline that modern editors of the *Tampa Tribune* would probably love to erase from the past of their publication. The newspaper's editor applauded a Tampa judge for his demand that Governor Trammell produce any law that would give administrators of the school a right to refuse very young children. There was no law to defend its desperate stand and the school was forced to open its doors to children of all ages. By forcing the issue, Hillsborough County officials opened the doors of the School for Boys to children as young as two. George Grissam was one of those that the school did its best to stop from being sent there.[4]

Concluding with Grissam, school records indicate that 18 students and 2 employees died at the school from its opening day in 1900 until October 15, 1918. The racial breakdown of the students reveals that 9 whites, 7 blacks and 2 students for whom no race was listed had passed away. Both of the deceased employees were white. This statistic shows that African American students, who comprised the majority of the juveniles sentenced to the school, were less likely to die there than their white counterparts.

George Grissam's death came just as the Spanish Influenza again reared its head in Florida. This time, however, it struck with a vengeance that instantly overwhelmed the best efforts of the state's doctors and public health officials. Reports prepared by the latter indicate that 371 Floridians lost their lives to the flu during a twelve-day period that ended on October 17, 1918. Jacksonville was placed on a city-wide quarantine and citizens were urged to wear masks. St. Augustine closed its schools, theaters and soda fountains while banning public gatherings and even church services. The month was remembered for years there as "churchless October."

The influenza spread like lightning and the best estimate is that 50% of Jackson County's citizens fell ill within a matter of days. The school, tragically, was not exempt.

The Great Flu Epidemic of 1918 is remembered today as the most severe and deadly pandemic ever to strike the United States. Estimates vary, but it is believed that between 500,000 and 650,000 Americans died from the influenza as did millions of people worldwide. The number of deaths from the Spanish influenza, in fact was higher than the number of battle deaths suffered in World War I.

The rate of sickness and speed with which the flu spread at the Florida Industrial School for Boys were stunning. Of the 267 students at the school when the influenza hit, 264 fell ill almost simultaneously. The assistant superintendent of the North or "colored" campus became sick, as did his entire family. All three of the schools engineers succumbed to the illness, as did all of the students that helped them run the school's power, water and sewage systems. With no one to run the pumps, the school's water dried up. With no water, the toilets and sinks no longer functioned. The small hospital, a wooden building measuring only 16 by 16 feet, was left without water or light.

The "colored" campus was overcrowded when the influenza struck and within three days, 196 of the 198 students and 8 of the 10 employees there fell ill. The matron of the North campus became the first person at the school to die. Her body laid unburied for almost 24 hours because there was no one to dig a grave. On the white or South campus, meanwhile, 68 of the 69 students became sick as did almost all of the employees.

Conditions deteriorated so quickly that "horror" is the only word to describe the situation there:

Conditions at the school are very bad. Sewerage imperfect, no sanitary rules at all, screens broke, fleas by the thousands. There were thirty-five cases of pneumonia, lack of medicine and lack of proper nourishment. No linen, boys lying under wool blankets, naked, with dirty mattresses on the cement floor; the reason said to be that the husks would all run out if put on a cot. The condition was one of filth, body lice, improper food, no bathing for lack of towels.[5]

Dr. George W. Klock, who wrote the above, was an official with the U.S. Public Health Service. He arrived at the school as influenza was still raging and conditions were at their worst:

The dinner of the well colored boys the day I was there being hoecake and bacon grease thickened with flour. The dinner of the white boys being rice and bacon grease gravy. One boy said he was flogged for refusing to cook peas full of worms; that meat sent to the boys was kept until spoiled and then fed them and they all were sick.[6]

Klock did not note in his report that the citizens of Marianna were also suffering from the flu. Only one of the city's doctors remained on his feet and was so overwhelmed that he simply could not care for the hundreds of patients pleading for his help. Most citizens were left to care for themselves as deaths multiplied across Jackson County. Graves dating from the fall of 1918 dot the landscape at cemeteries throughout the area. Many of them contain the remains of children.

Eleven students and one employee died at the Florida Industrial School for Boys during the 1918 Spanish Influenza pandemic. Although the University of South Florida, citing a *Miami Herald* report, claimed that all were African American, school records indicate that both white and black students were among the deceased:

Wilbur Smith, 1918; Influenza; African American; Student
Willie Adkins; 1918; Influenza; African American; Student
Lloyd Dutton; 1918; Influenza; White; Student
Hilton Finley, 1918; Influenza; White; Student
Puner Warner; 1918; Influenza; White; Student
Ralph Whidden, 1918, Influenza, White, Student

Unknown, 1918, Influenza, Race unknown, Student
Unknown, 1918, Influenza, Race unknown, Student
Unknown, 1918, Influenza, Race unknown, Student
Unknown, 1918, Influenza, Race unknown, Student
Unknown, 1918, Influenza, Race unknown, Student
Unknown, 1918, Influenza, African American, Female Employee

Governor Sidney Catts ordered an investigation of conditions at the school. A group of three physicians carried out this inquiry and issued a report in January 1919 that scalded Dr. Klock for his failure to better investigate the causes of the horrific conditions he witnessed:

...Did Dr. Klock say that the superintendent was not a well man? That the assistant superintendent, in charge of the colored department, with all his family were stricken? Did he say that one of the matrons died and remained for hours without attention because the few not in bed had to give aid to the living? Did he say that the attending physician, the only doctor on his feet in Marianna and surrounding community had ten times as much to do as any human being could perform? Did he say that the school was without water for lack of help to run the pump, causing the sewers to choke? Did he say that sixty-eight out of sixty-nine white boys and one hundred and ninety-eight colored boys were down practically at one time? Did he say that the dining room...with cement floor, was temporarily converted into a hospital by a physician, to relieve the congestion in their dormitory?..Did he say that the good people of Marianna had been acting as nurses of this institution until the needs of their own families and surroundings took them away?[7]

The flu epidemic in Jackson County continued into 1919, but gradually faded away. As it eased in the community at large, it also eased at the school. The impact of the sickness, however, continued to be felt in the area for decades to come. Not only did many families lose loved ones, but children still in the womb at the time later suffered from a much higher rate of learning and physical disabilities than children born just one year later.

The Tampa media used the horror of the outbreak to resume its call that the school be closed. The *Tampa Tribune*, in fact, went so far as to call for the impeachment of any judge who sentenced a juvenile to the school:

The Tribune calls on the governor to order the immediate arrest of those in immediate charge, the suspension of any and all boards or commissions charged with knowing conditions there, and to release, or send to some other institution, every boy, black and white, at the Marianna reform school, until the promises to make it a safe and decent place are carried out.

And The Tribune declares that any judge, or other officer having the power, who sentences a boy to that place until it has been cleaned up, and until the judiciary of the state have seen that the guilty ones are punished, should be impeached at once.[8]

Other newspapers followed suit, but their demands fell on deaf ears. The Florida Legislature in December approved $25,000 to pay off the indebtedness of the school and fund the completion of the new buildings under construction there.

Several additional deaths took place at the school during the following two years, a time when the vestiges of the Spanish influenza still claimed many lives in the United States. Joseph C. Anderson, a young African American student, died in 1919. The cause of his death was not listed in the records, but influenza and pneumonia remained serious issues at that time. Leonard Simmons, race unknown, died on May 9, 1919, and was buried in the school cemetery. The next reported death was of Nathaniel Sawyer, race unknown, who died on December 12, 1920. He also was buried in the school cemetery.[9]

Sawyer's death closed out the deadliest decade in the school's history. Thirty people – both students and employees – died at the school in 1911-1920. When the two students and Superintendent Morgan who passed away prior to 1911 are added to this tally, it is clear that at least 33 people died at the school during its first two decades of operation. Of this number, 29 were students and 4 – or roughly 12 percent – were employees. More than two-thirds of them were buried in the Dozier School Cemetery.

Name	Cause	Year	Burial

Unknown	Exposure	1900-1906	Unknown
Unknown	Heart	1900-1906	Unknown
Burrell Morgan	Illness	6/3/1910	Marianna
Unknown	Unknown	1911	Unknown
Bennett Evans Employee	Fire	11/18/1914	Cemetery
Charles Evans Employee	Fire	11/18/1914	Cemetery
Joe Wethersbee	Fire	11/18/1914	Cemetery
Walter Fisher	Fire	11/18/1914	Cemetery
Clarence Parrott	Fire	11/18/1914	Cemetery
Louis Fernandez	Fire	11/18/1914	Cemetery
Harry Wells	Fire	11/18/1914	Cemetery
Clifford Jefford	Fire	11/18/1914	Cemetery
Waldo Drew Body Not Recovered	Fire	11/18/1914	Unrecovered
Scott Martin	Unknown	1915	Unknown
Granville Rogers	Unknown	1915	Unknown
Willie Fisher	Unknown	1915	Unknown
Sim Williams	Unknown	2/28/1916	Unknown
Tillman Mohind	Unknown	5/25/1916	Unknown

James Joshua	Unknown	1916	Unknown
Thomas Aikins	Unknown	4/16/1918	Unknown
Lee Gaalsby	Unknown	10/6/1918	Unknown
George Grissam	Chronic Gastritis	10/23/1918	Cemetery
Wilbur Smith	Influenza	1918	Cemetery
Willie Adkins	Influenza	1918	Cemetery
Lloyd Dutton	Influenza	1918	Cemetery
Hilton Finley	Influenza	1918	Cemetery
Puner Warner	Influenza	1918	Cemetery
Ralph Whidden	Influenza	1918	Cemetery
Unknown	Infuenza	1918	Cemetery
Unknown	Influenza	1918	Cemetery
Unknown	Influenza	1918	Cemetery
Unknown	Influenza	1918	Cemetery
Unknown	Influenza	1918	Cemetery
Unknown Employee	Influenza	1918	Cemetery
Joseph Anderson	Unknown	1919	Unknown
Leonard Simmons	Unknown	5/9/1919	Cemetery

Nathaniel Sawyer   Unknown   12/12/1920   Cememetery

---

[1] FDLE Report, Page 13.

[2] FDLE Report

[3] "3 Pickaninnies Have No Existence In Law," *Tampa Tribune*, June 17, 1914, Page 5.

[4] *Ibid.*

[5] Report of Dr. George W. Klock, U.S. Public Health Service, reprinted in *Tampa Tribune*, November 2, 1918.

[6] *Ibid.*

[7] Report of the Physicians' Committee to the Commissioners of the Board of State Institutions, Marianna, Florida, November 5, 1918.

[8] *Tampa Tribune*, November 1918.

[9] FDLE Report, pp. 8-14.

Four

Deaths in the early 1920s

THE DEATH RATE AT THE FLORIDA INDUSTRIAL SCHOOL FOR BOYS continued to be a serious problem as it entered its third decade of operation. While the school did not suffer another catastrophe like the 1914 fire or 1918 Spanish influenza outbreak, it continued to see young men die from illness and other causes.

Wallace Ward died of pneumonia in 1921 and was carried home to Walton County for burial. Arthur Williams died on February 26, 1921. The school ledger does not list the cause of his death but notes that he was buried in the cemetery at "Boot Hill."[1]

A bit more is known about the death of John H. Williams, which took place on July 9, 1921. He was digging with two other students in the clay or "lime" pit associated with the school's brick plant when a wall gave way. All three were buried alive in the collapse, but frantic rescue efforts managed to save two of the boys. Williams, however, suffocated before he could be pulled from the earth. The loss of John H. Williams in July 1921 took place at a time when state authorities learned of alleged improprieties by administrators of the institution.[2]

A state investigation conducted in 1921 found that Superintendent Dr. Frank E. McClane and Assistant Superintendent M.A. Garrard had used labor provided by the students of Florida Industrial School to enrich themselves. The two men made arrangements with the First National Bank in Marianna to finance the acquisition of property held by the bank. They then took boys from the school out to their private lands to cut the large timber growing there. The logs were hauled back to the school and sawed into lumber at the state-owned sawmill. The two administrators then sold the boards to several buyers – including the State of Florida. The men made $9,320.33 from the state alone between January 20, 1920 and May 15, 1921 while at the same time reducing their costs by using juvenile offenders as unpaid laborers and allowing themselves free use of state equipment and facilities, including the school sawmill.[3]

When news of these activities exploded in Tallahassee, state-wide controversy was the result. Newspaper editors targeted the two administrators and political pressure against them grew from every corner of the state. Summoned before the state Board of Institutions, McClane and Garrard resigned. Criminal charges were not pursued against them.[4]

The next death reported at the institution was that of Guy Hudson, a white male who died while swimming with other boys on August 14, 1921. It took rescuers two days to recover his body. Hudson was from Milton and the school ledger reflects that his family arranged for his body to be shipped home. This was handled by the local funeral home and he was returned to Santa Rosa County for burial.[5]

State prisons and institutions were often the nearest places where the public could find emergency medical care during the early decades of the 20th century. The Florida State Hospital in Chattahoochee, for example, had a ward dedicated for treatment of the general public. The Florida Industrial School also made its infirmary available to the general public when a citizen was in need of emergency care. In those days when most citizens still traveled by mule and wagon, it could take hours to reach the nearest hospital or doctor and access to the nurses and physicians at state facilities saved many lives. This is likely the reason that in 1921 a local farmer showed up at the campus infirmary with an unconscious young man named Samuel Morgan. He died while the medical staff there worked to revive him.

Census data shows that Morgan was born in either 1894 or 1896, which would make him either 25 or 27 years old when he was rushed to the school. He had once been a student at the Florida Industrial School, but had been paroled as required by state law when he was 21. After Morgan turned 22, he no longer could be returned to the school and he was regarded by law as a citizen of Florida with all rights restored. The young man, however, continued to live with the farm family to which he had been paroled when he left the school. This decision by Morgan might seem unusual, but when the circumstances of his life are reviewed, his choice seems quite logical.[6]

Samuel Morgan spent his early childhood at Fort Denaud, a community in Lee County, Florida, that was named for military post that stood there during the Seminole Wars. In 1910 he was one of six children living with his father, Ephraim Morgan. Their mother, Helen Morgan, had died and Ephraim was a widower. The children included two girls and four boys and ranged in age from 7 to 17.[7]

Something happened in the Morgan home between 1910 and 1920, for by the latter date Ephraim Morgan was living alone in Fort Denaud and all of the children were gone. Samuel Morgan by then had already been sentenced to and paroled from the Florida Industrial School for Boys. His sister, Annie, married a farmer named William Benjamin Johnson prior to 1919. The couple was living in Centralia, a community in Hernando County, by 1920. They later relocated to Hillsborough County.[8]

It was common practice in those days for the school to parole students either to their families or to individuals that could help them transition to employment in the trade that they had earned on campus. Agriculture was a major part of the school and its training programs and Morgan had shown proficiency in farming. For some reason he chose not to be paroled to his father in Fort Denaud but instead accepted an offer of employment with a local family near Marianna. When he turned 22 and was no longer under parole, he decided to stay.

He was still working as a farm laborer when he became deathly ill and collapsed in 1921. The nature of his illness is not known, but records of the Jackson County Commission show that there was a surge in illness and death during the fall of that year, just as there had been each fall since 1917. The county experienced a dramatic increase in costs for medical care, medicines and coffins due to a dramatic increase in sickness at the Jackson County Jail during the fall of 1921. The situation was so serious that the commissioners authorized the hiring of a county doctor for the first time on January 11, 1922.[9]

Samuel "Sam" Morgan died between August and December 1921, when this surge in illness was at its peak. The Jackson County Grand Jury did not investigate his death, although it investigated some previous deaths at the school such as those suffered during the 1914 fire. Neither did the Jackson County Coroner's Jury, which also had investigated previous deaths including those

35

from the fatal fire. This indicates that it was likely the opinion of county officials that Morgan's death was the result of illness and that he had died while receiving medical care.[10]

Although he was no longer a student, Morgan was buried in the school cemetery on "Boot Hill."

The death rate at the school dropped significantly from 1921 to 1922. The first death in 1922 took place on April 15 when Schley Hunter, a white student, died from pneumonia. His next of kin was the school's superintendent and he was buried in the cemetery on "Boot Hill." The second person to die that year was Calvin Williams, an African American student, who died on December 31. His cause of death was not listed in school records but he was buried in the cemetery.[11]

The death rate dropped again in 1923 with only one fatal sickness reported at the school. George W. Chancey, Jr., a white male, died from malaria. His next of kin was listed as Superintendent Knight, an indication that he had no known living relatives, and he was buried in the school cemetery.[12]

Two students died in 1924, Clifford Miller and Charles Frank Overstreet. Both were African Americans. Little is known about the circumstances of Miller's death, although he was likely buried in the school cemetery. Overstreet died while having tonsillectomy surgery on August 19, 1924. His next of kin was Mamie James. At the time the next of kin of a student that died at the Florida Industrial School could have their loved one buried in the campus cemetery, come to Marianna and retrieve the body in person, or pay for a funeral home to ship the body home for burial. Charles Overstreet was buried in the cemetery at "Boot Hill."[13]

Three students died in 1925. Edward Fonders died in an accidental drowning on May 18, 1925. He was buried in the school cemetery. Walter Askew died from unspecified causes on December 18, 1925, and was also buried at "Boot Hill." The third student to die in 1925 was Thomas Curry. His case will be discussed in the next chapter.[14]

[1] Florida Industrial School Ledgers, Florida State Archives.

[2] *Tampa Tribune*, September 1, 1921, p. 4.

[3] *Ibid.*

[4] *Ibid.*

[5] Florida Industrial School Ledgers, Florida State Archives; Tampa Tribune, September 1, 1921, p. 4; Marianna Times-Courier, August 19, 1921.

[6] United States Census for Lee County Florida, 1900; United States Census for Lee County, Florida, 1910; Note: Florida law required that students from the Florida Industrial School for Boys be released by their 22nd birthday.

[7] United States Census for Lee County, Florida, 1910.

[8] United States Census for Lee County, Florida, 1920; United States Census for Hernando County Florida, 1920; Florida State Census for Hillsborough County, Florida, 1935.

[9] County Commission Minutes Book, 1918-1922, Jackson County Archives.

[10] Circuit Court Minutes, Jackson County Archives; Jackson County Coroner's Inquest records, Jackson County Archives.

[11] Florida Industrial School Ledgers, Florida State Archives.

[12] *Ibid.*

[13] *Ibid.*

[14] *Ibid.*

SCHOOL BAND IN 1920S (NOTICE THAT IT WAS DESEGREGATED)

CLAY PIT (#13), SCENE OF A TRAGIC DEATH

Five

Thomas Curry & the late 1920s

RESEARCHERS FROM THE UNIVERSITY OF SOUTH FLORIDA once again ignited a media frenzy on October 7, 2014, when they unearthed a coffin in Philadelphia, Pennsylvania. They expected the wooden box to contain the remains of Thomas Curry, an escapee from the Florida Industrial School for Boys. No traces of a body were found.

Curry had walked away from the unfenced campus on December 10, 1925. He fell through the railroad trestle over the Apalachicola River at River Junction, a community adjoining Chattahoochee, the next day. Rushed to the public ward of the Florida State Hospital for care, he died soon after.

The USF team had long wanted to exhume his purported grave in Pennsylvania. U.S. Senator Bill Nelson threw his support behind the idea and officials in Pennsylvania helped locate Curry's living family members – who admitted they knew little about him – so that the university's scientists could help bring them closure. The university's media relations staff helped orchestrate massive news coverage and the team set off to exhume an 89-year-old grave in one of America's leading media markets.[1]

The discovery that there were no apparent human remains in the unmarked grave – which also contained the coffins of other family members – ignited a predictable media explosion. Newspapers and television stations around the world published details under a variety of sensational headlines:

> "Infamous Florida reform school sent family coffin full of
> word instead of son's body" – WXIN-TV

"Casket belonging to boy killed at horror reform school in 1925 found empty" – *The New York Daily News*

"Dead Boy's Coffin Found Empty In Investigation Of Sadistic Florida Reform School" – Inquisitor.com

"Nightmare Fla. School sends family an empty coffin" – Examiner.com

"Two More added to Florida prisons' sadistic legacy" – *Miami Herald*

"Thomas Curry's Body Missing From Coffin, Likely Located at Mass Gravesite At Former Dozier School For Boys" – IMDb.com

Hundreds of other newspapers, television stations and websites followed suit. Not one of the hundreds of media outlets that blasted out such sensational headlines bothered to search the records to find out what really happened to Curry's remains and who was responsible for the empty coffin in Philadelphia. If they had, they would have found that the evidence shows that the Florida Industrial School for Boys was not involved in shipping the coffin involved in the "empty grave" situation.

Thomas Curry, a native of Philadelphia, was around 15 years old when he was sentenced to the Florida Industrial School for Boys in 1925 by a judge in Dade County, Florida. The school at that time was not fenced and had just passed a medical inspection by Dr. J.H. Colson of Tallahassee. He reported to the Board of Commissioners of State Institutions that the "health of the inmates as a whole was good, and they seemed happy and contented."[2]

Dr. Colson had visited the school in late February 1925 and reported that recent influenza cases there were controlled and that conditions were good:

The sanitary conditions of the buildings and grounds are good. The food is plentiful and well prepared, and everything working harmoniously so far as I was able to observe.

Most of the inmates are employed and required to work according to respective adaptability to the kind of work suitable to them.[3]

Dr. Colson noted that the population of the school at the time of his visit consisted of 190 white juveniles on the South Campus and 191 "colored" juveniles on the North Campus. They were, he noted, "properly cared for, well clothed and well fed."[4]

The doctor's inspection was one in a series conducted by state authorities in the years after the deadly 1918 flu outbreak. Elected officials in Tallahassee were still smarting from the editorial outrage that had been directed at them due to the influenza deaths and conditions under which the sick boys had been suffering at that time.

It has not been mentioned in the widespread coverage of his case, but Thomas Curry had reason to be worried in December 1925. One of his friends had just been subpoenaed by attorneys in Miami to return there and testify against the Sheriff of Dade County and two of his deputies. Curry likely had real reason to fear that he would be next.

The case revolved around an escape conspiracy at the Dade County Jail and the gunning down of inmates by the sheriff and other officers. It was best summarized by Circuit Judge A.J. Rose when he gave instructions for an investigation to the Dade County Grand Jury:

I call your attention to the killing, by the sheriff or his deputies, of two men and the serious wounding of a number of men on Sunday, September 27, in the jail yard at Miami. It is reported that the sheriff knew several days before the killing that prisoners in the jail would attempt to escape on the Sunday morning and that he knew the hour at which the escape would be made. It is said that with that knowledge the sheriff made no attempt to frustrate the escape, but that he stationed armed deputies about the jail yard, where they could not be seen by the escaping prisoners. It is reported that the sheriff knew that the prisoners who did attempt to escape were all unarmed and with that knowledge, that he or his deputies shot down and killed two prisoners and wounded a number of others. This is a serious matter and I charge you that it demands a most thorough and painstaking investigation of the facts.[5]

Sheriff Henry Chase of Dade County and two of his deputies were charged with 2nd Degree Murder in the case. Five other deputies and six Miami police officers were charged with being accessories to murder.[6]

One of the key witnesses called by prosecutors was Oliver Grady, a student at the Florida Industrial School for Boys. The youth had been in the Dade County Jail with several other juveniles awaiting transport to the school when the shooting took place. They saw and heard the bloody assault. Grady was subpoenaed to testify against the powerful sheriff and 13 other law enforcement officers.[7]

The news that a student had been subpoenaed to testify at the trial and against so many officers of the law must have send shock waves through the population of the school when it reached campus during the second week of December. Boys that had come to the school from Dade County must have been especially impacted if not terrified by the news, wondering if they would be the next to be summoned. Among these was Thomas Curry, who slipped away from the school that week.

The timing of Curry's escape raises serious questions as to his motives for running. The teenager's decision to run precisely as news spread that a student sentenced from Dade County had been called to testify against that county's sheriff and other high profile officers is unlikely to have been coincidental. Ironically, the *Miami Herald*, which made much of the exhumation of Thomas Curry's alleged coffin, made no mention of how more than one dozen of its city's and county's law enforcement officers had admittedly gunned down unarmed inmates during the same year.

A search was conducted for the young runaway, but he could not be found. How long it took for school employees to notice his absence is not known. What is known is that the youth made his way east, either by hopping a train or following the L&N (now CSX) railroad tracks that connected Marianna with all points east.

By the morning of November 11, 1925, Curry was in the Sneads vicinity, still following the railroad tracks. His route of travel brought him to the long railroad bridge and trestle over the Apalachicola River between Sneads and River Junction. The river itself has been a barrier to foot travel for thousands of years. Wide and deep, it separates the high bluffs to the east from the rich farmlands and swamps to the west. The L&N tracks cross the river at a point where there are floodplain swamps on each side, taking advantage of the

Mosquito Creek lowlands on the east side to avoid the need for a deep cut into the rocky face of the high bluffs. While this route reduced the amount of work required for the crews that built the railroad during the late 1800s, it did necessitate the construction of long approach trestles on each side of the river. Because the main bridge over the river had to be high enough for the tall stacks of paddlewheel steamboats to pass underneath, the approach trestles had to be very high as well.

The curve of the western approach of the railroad to the river and the length of the bridge and trestles meant that Curry could not see from one end of the elevated crossing to the other. This created an extremely dangerous situation for him because if a train approached from either direction while he was walking across, he would not be able to outrun it. The combined length of the bridge and its approach trestles is more than 1.5 miles.[8]

Despite the danger, Thomas Curry started across the Apalachicola and its floodplain swamps by walking along the tracks of the L&N Railroad. He made it across the Jackson County approach trestle and the main bridge over the river itself. As he walked along atop the trestle on the Gadsden County side, however, he either saw or heard the sound of an approaching train. Curry tried to run but missed a step and fell through between two of the crossties on the elevated trestle.

He was within sight of River Junction, a community that adjoins the historic old city of Chattahoochee, when he fell. A major freight yard was located there in 1925 where cargo from paddlewheel riverboats could be loaded into freight cars and vice versa. The community was also home to a large brick yard.

Workers in River Junction witnessed Curry's tumble from the tracks and rushed to his aide. They found him on the ground at the base of the trestle and realized he had sustained massive head injuries in his fall. Loading him into a vehicle, they carried him up the hill and into Chattahoochee to the Florida State Hospital. Now noted as a mental health facility, the hospital also had a public ward in its early days. Dr. B.F. Barnes was on duty that day.[9]

Dr. Barnes and other medical professionals at the hospital administered emergency care to the youth in a desperate attempt to save his life. The Florida State Hospital had some of the best equipment and facilities in North Florida but Curry's injuries were so severe that there was little the doctor and nurses could do to help him. He died shortly after arriving at FSH.[10]

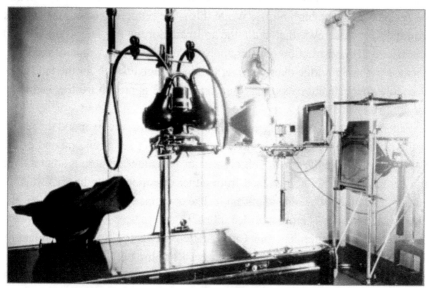

EXAM ROOM AT FLORIDA STATE HOSPITAL, 1920S.

BRIDGE OVER THE APALACHICOLA WHERE THOMAS CURRY FELL IN 1925.

A coroner's inquest was convened and Gadsden County authorities determined that the teenager had died as a result of his fall from the railroad trestle. The *Gadsden County Times*, a Quincy newspaper, reported at the time that Curry "died from the effect of a crushing blow on the forehead received when he hit the ground or a timber." This was also the conclusion reported in the Boys School ledger books, which note that Curry was "killed on R.R. bridge in Chattahoochee, Fla. Dec. 11, 1925."[11]

The source for both the Quincy newspaper and the administrative staff at the school was Dr. Barnes. He also signed the boy's death certificate, which cited the Gadsden County's Coroner's Jury verdict that Curry "came to his death from a wound in forehead; skull crushed from an unknown cause." The death certificate also indicates that the teenager lived for about 30 minutes before dying at the state hospital.[12]

The University of South Florida and media have made much of the "unknown cause" notation on Curry's death certificate, but apparently did not look at other eyewitness testimony about his death. Dr. Barnes, who treated the youth and tried to save his life, was clear that the injury was caused when the youth fell through the trestle and hit his forehead on "the ground or a timber." The "unknown cause" determination by the Coroner's Jury simply meant that they weren't sure whether striking the ground or one of the heavy wooden bridge timbers had led to Curry's fatal injury. There was no doubt by either Dr. Barnes or the Coroner that the young man's death was caused by a fall from the tracks.[13]

The *Gadsden County Times* made this clear in its issue of December 24, 1925:

Dr. B.F. Barnes, member of the medical staff of the State hospital at Chattahoochee, was in the city yesterday and gave out some further information in relation to the unfortunate youth, Thos. E. Curry, who died from the effects of a fall through the railroad trestle on the eastern approach to the bridge across the Apalachicola near River Junction.[14]

The surviving records and media reports from 1925 indicate that there was neither confusion nor mystery about the cause of Curry's death. His fall from the tracks had been witnessed and he had died while in the care of medical professionals. In addition, it was very clear that the only connection between his death and the Florida Industrial School for Boys was the fact that he had run away from that facility the previous day. Some media reports in 2014 suggested that he had died while running from school employees or while being chased by vicious "dog teams." Neither of these insinuations was true. The oft-mentioned "dog teams" operated from the Apalachee Correctional Institution in Sneads, a facility that did not even exist in 1925. And the claims that he was running from school employees at the moment he fell are not substantiated by the records of the Coroner's inquest.[15]

In other words, over the top headlines such as the 2014 claim by the *New York Daily News* that Thomas Curry was "killed at horror reform school" are not supported by any of the original documentation. The railroad trestle where he fell is nearly 25 miles from the campus.

The surviving documentation also shows that Thomas Curry's body was not returned to Marianna and that the "Infamous Florida Reform School" was not involved in its preparation or shipping:

His body was embalmed and efforts made to ascertain his home and parentage. After his death a letter address to him was received at the reform school, which was given to Dr. Barnes. It was from his grandmother in Philadelphia and enclosed a small sum of money to him and was of a kind but reproachful tone and full of good advice.[16]

Using the return address on the envelope, Dr. Barnes was able to make contact with Susanna O'Connell, the teenager's widowed grandmother. His parents – to whom WXIN-TV (Indianapolis) claimed the school sent a box of wood instead of their "son's body" – were no longer alive. Mrs. O'Connell was the boy's maternal grandmother. His father and mother had died in a murder suicide when he was a young child.[17]

Mrs. O'Connell wanted her grandson's remains sent home. Throughout this time his body had remained in the morgue at the Florida State Hospital, not at the school in Marianna as many have claimed. As was the case at the school, the staff at Florida State Hospital would arrange to have a private funeral home ship home the body of a loved one at a family's expense. If the next of kin could not afford this, they could come and retrieve the body in person or it would be buried in the state cemetery. The records of the Florida State Hospital do not indicate the presence of a grave that could be that of Thomas Curry.

Instead, the records indicate that Dr. Barnes made arrangements with Mrs. O'Connell for a private funeral home in Chattahoochee to handle her grandson's remains. Curry's death certificate shows that the 15-year-old's body was turned over to a private mortician on December 26, 1925, the same day that some believe he was buried at Old Cathedral Cemetery in Philadelphia. The document specifically notes the day after Christmas as the "date of removal" of the body from the state morgue.[18]

What happened to Curry's body from there is a mystery. USF found no bones in his alleged grave in Philadelphia, although the university's researchers did find more than just wood in the coffin. They also found straw or grass of some type and what appeared to be the remains of a funeral wreath. Some media outlets – including the *Tampa Bay Times* – reported that thumbscrews on the wooden box or coffin in the grave were "identical" to those used at the Dozier School Cemetery, but researchers told other outlets that the hardware was "similar." This is reasonable as most pauper's coffins were probably prepared in a similar manner in that day and age.

The presence of a funeral wreath inside the coffin or box indicates that it was opened at some time, most likely after it arrived in Philadelphia as no such ornamentation would have accompanied the body at the Florida State Hospital morgue. Was his body removed at that time? Was he cremated? Was he actually buried in Florida and the funeral in Pennsylvania simply a memorial service? No one knows the answer. What is clear, however, is that a private funeral home and neither Florida State Hospital nor the Florida Industrial School for Boys had possession of the body when it was last seen and documented.

The funeral home burned several decades ago and its records – which might have shed light on the mystery – are believed to have been destroyed.

The death rate at the Florida Industrial School itself continued to decline in the second five years of the 1920s. Willie Sherman and George Johnson both died in 1926, but the only other information available is that they were buried off campus. Daniel Nollie Davis, a white student, died of pneumonia on February 8, 1926. Superintendent Knight was listed as his next of kin and he was buried in the school cemetery. One death – Earnest Mobley, who was buried off campus – was reported in 1927. One additional death – Moses Roberts, who also was buried off campus – was reported in 1928. Then in 1929, three deaths were reported. Robert B. Rhoden, an African American student, died of pneumonia on May 8, 1929. His next of kin was Annie Walton but he was not returned home for burial and was interred instead in the cemetery on "Boot Hill." Samuel Bethel, also African American, died of tuberculosis on October 15, 1929. He had no known next of kin and was also buried at "Boot Hill."[19]

The final death in 1929 was also the school's first confirmed homicide. A student doused James C. Ansley with gasoline and set him afire in what school officials labeled a "hazing" incident. He died on October 19, 1929:

Gasoline was thrown upon Ansley by another youth, whose name was not given, the board was told, and then ignited. The incident occurred in the printing department of the institution. Efforts were made to extinguish the blaze, but Ansley ran away from his would be rescuers, his clothing ablaze.

Ansley, who was serving a sentence from Marion county, died from the burns three days later, after it had seemed he would recover.

An investigation of the occurrence was sought by the board when Commissioner of Agriculture Nathan Mayo member of the board from whose home county Ansley was sent to the institution, was told that the burning was the result of a "hazing" inflicted upon the lad.[20]

The name of the student responsible for Ansley's death was never identified and no charges were filed in the incident. Superintendent W.A. Vanlandingham described the tragic incident as a "prank" gone bad. It was the first time in the three decade history of the school that a human death could positively be said to have been caused by another person. Allegations were raised about the 1914 fire, but the Jackson County Grand Jury declined to indict the man suspected of setting the fatal blaze.[21]

Ansley's body was returned home to Marion County for burial.[22]

The years 1926-1929 ended with these four additional deaths reported at the school. Three were the result of illness and one resulted from a hazing incident. Three of the unfortunate students were buried in the school cemetery at "Boot Hill." One was returned home for burial.

[1] Condensed scenario based on emails sent to and from an array of USF employees, obtained by the author using Florida's Sunshine Law and Public Records statutes.

[2] Florida Industrial School for Boys Ledgers, Florida State Archives; Dr. J.H. Colson, Report to Dr. Fons Hathaway, Secretary to the Commissioners of the Board of State Institutions, February 1925.

[3] *Ibid.*

[4] *Ibid.*

[5] Hon. A.J. Rose, Circuit Judge, Instructions to the Grand Jury of Dade County, Florida, October 5, 1925.

[6] "Chase on Trial Today," *Miami Herald*, December 14, 1925.

[7] *Ibid.*

[8] Chattahoochee Quadrangle, Florida-Georgia, 7.5 Minute Series (Topographic) Map, U.S. Geological Survey, Washington, D.C., 1952.

[9] Coroner's Inquest Minutes, Death of Thomas Curry, December 11-12, 1945.

[10] *Ibid.*

[11] "Body of Boy Killed by Falling from Trestle Near River Junc'n Sent to Phila.," *Gadsden County Times*, December 24, 1925, Page 1.

[12] Death Certificate of Thomas Curry, 17448-422, December 13, 1925.

[13] *Ibid.*, Coroner's Inquest Minutes, Death of Thomas Curry, December 11-12, 1925; "Body of Boy Killed by Falling from Treste Near River Junc'n Sent to Phila.," *Gadsden County Times*, December 24, 1925, Page 1 (hereafter *Gadsden County Times*, December 24, 1925, Page 1).

[14] *Gadsden County Times*, December 24, 1925, Page 1.

[15] Coroner's Inquest Minutes, Death of Thomas Curry, December 11-12, 1925.

[16] *Gadsden County Times*, December 24, 1925, Page 1.

[17] "Wife Slayer Dying," *Philadelphia Inquirer*, January 3, 1916, Page 13; "Man Who Killed Wife Dies," *Philadelphia Inquirer*, January 4, 1916, Page 6.

[18] Death Certificate of Thomas Curry, 17448-422, December 13, 1925 (shipping notation dated December 26, 1925).

[19] Florida Industrial School for Boys Ledgers, Florida State Archives.

[20] *Polk County Record*, October 29, 1929, p. 2.

[21] *Ibid.*; Circuit Court Minutes, Jackson County Archives.

[22] Florida Industrial School for Boys Ledgers, Florida State Archives.

Six

Deaths in the 1930s

THE YEARS 1930-1939 BEGAN WITH SIGNS OF IMPROVEMENT in the death rate at the Florida Industrial School for Boys. No deaths were reported in 1930-1931, a promising change from 1929 when three boys died. Everything changed, however, in 1932. Nineteen students died at the school by the end of the decade, most in 1932. Most were African American and most succumbed to illness. One, however, was the victim of the school's first recorded murder.

The school's first death of the 1930s took place on January 5, 1932. Lee Smith, an African American student, died that day in a horrible farm accident:

A sad occurrence of Tuesday, January 5, was the death of Lee Smith, fifteen year old colored boy, which came about through an accident while the boys were making their way from the field during the dinner hour. The boy was riding on one of two mules hitched together when he slipped off between them, catching his foot in the trace chain where he was unable to get loose before the mule gave a lurch which broke the bridle, and further exciting it into running.

With the bridal off it was a hard job to stop the mule which made a straight course for the gate estimated to be about four hundred yards away, here stopping of its own free will. The boy was picked up and carried to the Baltzell hospital where he died from internal injuries.[1]

The Baltzell Hospital was a privately-owned hospital at the intersection of Lafayette and Russ Streets in Marianna. Patients of all races were treated there,

53

even during the Jim Crow era. Lee Smith was carried back to the school following his death and buried in the school cemetery.

Another death followed on February 11, 1932, when white student named Lonnie Frank Harrell died while in surgery for a hernia repair. He was returned home to Hillsborough County and is buried at Orange Hill Cemetery in Tampa. Harrell was the second student to die during surgery. Charles Frank Overstreet had died while receiving a tonsillectomy in 1924.[2]

And then came the influenza. The flu was deadly and feared during the early decades of the 20th century. While it did not reach the proportions of the Great Flu of 1918, another deadly outbreak spread across the South in 1932. The Great Depression was then underway and even when medical help was available, many people could not afford to pay for it.

The influenza of 1932 first surfaced in late winter and early spring. It seemed at first to target children in greater numbers than adults. City health authorities in Dallas, Texas, reported in February that nearly 800 children were out of school due to the outbreak. Dr. J.W. Bass, the city's Health Director, urged residents to call a physician and go immediately to bed at the first sign of flu symptoms. National health officials reported by May 5 that 9,000 cases of influenza were being treated in the United States. [3]

The influenza struck at the Florida Industrial School for Boys much as it had in 1918, spreading first through the North or "colored" campus

For the past three weeks a siege of influenza has been raging among the boys on the colored side, causing most of the work to be shut down, and every precaution possible taken to keep it from spreading to the boys on the white side.

Over one hundred boys have been in bed so far with the flu and twenty eight more are still in the hospital at the present time, according to Mr. Marmaduke Dickson, superintendent of the colored boys. The epidemic has been of a very serious nature, with some of the boys' cases turning into pneumonia, regardless of the careful treatment they are receiving.[4]

School classes were closed at the school and both the education building and officers' club room were converted to temporary sleeping quarters in order to further separate the boys from each other in hopes of slowing the spread of the illness.[5]

COTTAGES IN 1932

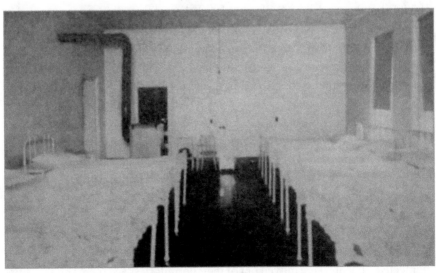

HOSPITAL AS IT APPEARED IN 1932

Despite such efforts, the flu once again was particularly deadly on the North Campus. Nine young men, all African American, died from influenza or flu-related pneumonia over the days and months that followed:[6]

NAME[7]	RACE	CAUSE OF DEATH
James Brinson	African-American	Pneumonia/Flu
Willie Heading	African-American	Pneumonia/Flu
Sam M. Nipper	African-American	Pneumonia/Flu
Jesse D. Denson	African-American	Pneumonia/Flu
Fred Sams	African-American	Influenza
Lee Underwood	African-American	Influenza
Dary Pender	African-American	Influenza
Archie Shaw	African-American	Influenza
Joe Stephens	African-American	Influenza

Only three of these unfortunate youth had next of kin other than school officials but due to the medical crisis it is believed that all nine were buried in the school cemetery on "Boot Hill." There is no indication that any of the remains were turned over to a funeral home for shipment.[8]

The influenza returned again in the fall and winter of 1932, but this time was not as dangerous as it has been in the spring:

Although it reached fairly extensive proportions as to the number of boys sick, the recent epidemic of influenza here has been termed extremely mild in every case by the School nurses and physicians. About 125 boys have been received and dismissed from the School hospital in cases of Flu, but no serious sickness has yet occurred. Not one of the cases was at all severe, and the epidemic seems to have definitely abated.[9]

The school hospital in 1932 was located in Cottage Number Four. All uninfected students were moved out of their dormitory space there and the entire structure reserved for the care of flu patients. This again allowed for more separation between the beds of those suffering from influenza. Dr. N.A. Baltzell remained in close attendance throughout the spell of sickness and this time no students died. At least one member of the medical staff, Mrs. Alva Moran, became sick with the flu. She was the full-time nurse that normally operated the hospital. Several other employees of the school also became sick.[10]

The influenza had completely abated by the end of the year. Mrs. Moran, now back in charge of the hospital, reported that the entire facility had been sanitized. She also noted in the school newspaper that she was able to spend Christmas with her family near Faceville, Georgia.[11]

One other student died in 1932, but not on campus. Oscar Elvis Murphy escaped from the school and was struck by an automobile in Hardee County, Florida. The institution was not involved in the incident and he was buried there near his home.[12]

By the end of the deadly year, twelve students of the Florida Industrial School for Boys had lost their lives. Nine died from the flu, one was killed by a mule while working on the school farm, one was struck by a car in Hardee County, and one died while undergoing surgery for a hernia repair.

No deaths were reported at the Florida Industrial School for Boys in 1933, a welcome respite after the deadly influenza outbreak the previous year. One of the more controversial deaths in the school's history, however, occurred the following year.

The individual involved in that circumstance was Thomas Varnadoe, a white student who was sentenced to the school with his brother after being arrested in Brooksville for malicious trespassing. He died of pneumonia at 2:51 p.m. on the afternoon of October 26, 1934:

Thomas had been in ill health for several years, but his health seemed to be arriving after his arrival at the school on September 22. On Sunday, October 21, he went to the school hospital complaining that he was feeling bad and was kept there and given medical attention. The little fellow's vitality was so greatly lowered from his protracted illness that he failed to respond readily to treatment and later developed pneumonia.

Thomas is the son of Mr. And Mrs. T.H. Varnadoe of Hernando county. Upon his arrival at the school he was placed in cottage One, and assigned to the Yard Crew for work. He has a brother, Herbert, in Cottage Three at the present time.

Funeral services were held on Saturday, October 27, at the school cemetery. Dr. C.B. Toombs, pastor of the First Presbyterian Church of Marianna conducted the services.

The Aces of the school acted as pall bearers, and a large number of the officers of the school were present.[13]

The 13-year-old's death became controversial many years later when his nephew, Glen Varnadoe, demanded that the teenager's remains be returned to his family. More than 75-years had passed since Thomas died at the school, but the location of his grave suddenly became front page news for the *Tampa Bay Times* and other media outlets.

No one in Marianna or Jackson County objected to Glen Varnadoe retrieving his uncle's remains. The issue was whether all of the graves should be disturbed in order to find one person without first obtaining the permission of the next of kin of other individuals buried in the cemetery. In fact, community representatives even called on the Secretary of the Department of Juvenile Justice to provide the family specific information on Thomas Varnadoe's grave location so his remains could be exhumed and turned over to his family. The University of South Florida (USF) reported in its interim report that a former student claimed that cemetery plats had existed on campus. Preserving all records from the school was the responsibility of the Department of Juvenile Justice and if such plats existed – as claimed by the university – then it should have been possible to identify Varnadoe's grave site. If not, then county leaders asked that other families be notified before their loved ones remains were disturbed.

In response to this, former students and the media outlets attempted to raise claims that the community was "hiding" something by not wanting all of the graves exhumed without the permissions of the next of kin. The *Tampa Bay Times* published a story under the headline "In Marianna, dig for truth encounters desire to keep past buried" that went so far as to include claims that the Dozier School campus was a dumping ground for the bodies of African Americans killed by the Ku Klux Klan (KKK). The writer, Ben Montgomery, offered no explanation as to why the Ku Klux Klan would take bodies to the nearest state facility for burial. Missing from his story was the fact that the Southern Poverty Law Center (SPLC) has identified no active Klan klaverns within 100 miles of Jackson County, Florida or that the organization has documented seven hate groups within the immediate Tampa Bay area.[14]

As the KKK allegation gained traction, even CNN entered the fray. Rich Phillips, a senior producer with the 24-hour cable network, cited anonymous claims in 2013 that the "Boot Hill" cemetery might contain the remains of African Americans buried there by the Ku Klux Klan. A newspaper in London went so far as to publish an article on the cemetery under a banner headline that proclaimed Dozier School was a "'A concentration camp for little boys': Dark secrets unearthed in KKK county."[15]

The closest any of these writers came to explaining how a known cemetery on the grounds of a state facility could somehow be a Ku Klux Klan dumping ground was in the *Tampa Bay Times* article, which noted that Thomas Varnadoe had died on October 26, 1934, the same day as the Claude Neal lynching in Jackson County. The reporter did not explain, however, that no one in Marianna knew of Neal's death until the following day.[16]

In truth, the Florida Attorney General's Office was quick to refute such claims. Statewide Prosecutor Nick Cox responded to the allegations in an email to the author on April 24, 2013. "Oh c'mon Dale!!!!" he wrote. "Do you really think I am supporting such comments?" So far as is known, none of the media outlets that published or aired the allegations bothered to seek out the statewide prosecutor's opinion regarding them.[17]

The University of South Florida, however, concluded that Varnadoe and other white students that died at the school must be buried in a second, hidden or "clandestine" cemetery. USF researchers reported that Glen Varnadoe visited the campus prior to its closure in an effort to locate his uncle's burial site. According to their version of his account, they were told by him that school officials showed him the "Boot Hill" cemetery but then took him to a second location on campus and pointed out a burial ground they said was likely to contain Thomas Varnadoe's remains. The researchers also cited other eyewitnesses, many of them former students, as evidence of multiple burial grounds on the campus and pointed out that the "practices of segregation" would not have allowed whites and African Americans to be buried together. The university's team apparently did not notice that Marianna's Riverside Cemetery contains the graves of both white and black individuals dating from the 1930s.[18]

Glen Varnadoe offered a slightly different account of his visit to the school in a private discussion with the author. At that time he indicated that while he could not remember the exact year of his visit he believed it was in the 1980s. A school official, he said, took him to the "Boot Hill" cemetery in a pickup truck. After viewing the memorial crosses there, Varnadoe said, they got back into the truck and drove to a second location. He volunteered, however, that the second location could really have been a different side of the first cemetery instead of a different burial ground. This disclaimer, if made to USF researchers, was not included in their interim report.[19]

Thomas Varnadoe, in fact, was not buried in a second hidden cemetery. His remains were found in a grave at the known "Boot Hill" cemetery, exactly where school records indicated the unfortunate student had been buried. Identified using DNA by researchers at the University of North Texas, his remains were found along-side other students, both black and white, buried in a coffin and interred according to standard mortuary and religious practices of the 1930s.[20]

The rate of death at the Florida Industrial School for Boys slowed dramatically during the second half of the 1930s. The next reported death at the school was that of a student named Joshua Backey. He died of blood poisoning in 1935. Two students, Richard Nelson and Robert Cato, died of pneumonia at the Baltzell Hospital in Marianna on February 23 and February 25, 1935, respectively. Both were buried in the school cemetery.[21]

Grady Huff, also a student, died of "acute nephritis" on March 4, 1935. The location of his death was given in the school newspaper as the F.I.S. Hospital. Acute nephritis is a severe inflammation of the kidney. As was the case with Thomas Varnadoe the previous year, Huff's death was reported in the school newspaper:

Funeral Services were held in the School cemetery on Tuesday, March 5th, at 11 a.m., with Dr. C.B. Toombs, Pastor of the First Presbyterian Church of Marianna, in charge. All of the boys of Cottage Two, the cottage where Grady lived, and all members of the laundry crew, the crew in which he worked, attended the funeral. Miss Inez Huff, of St. Petersburg, sister of the deceased, and a large number of Staff members also attended the services.[22]

Dr. Toombs, the pastor that conducted the services for Huff, was the same minister called on to officiate at the funeral of Thomas Varnadoe in 1934. The presence of Huff's sister at the funeral proves that family members sometimes attended burials at the "Boot Hill" cemetery.

The next death reported was that of James or Joseph Hammond. He died of tuberculosis on May 2, 1936, but it is not clear whether he was on campus at the time. Victims of tuberculosis were usually quarantined in sanitariums or special tuberculosis hospitals at that time due to the highly contagious nature of the disease. His next of kin was listed in the ledgers as "F.I.S." (Florida Industrial School) and it is possible but not certain that he was buried at "Boot Hill."[23]

The last death to occur at the school during the 1930s resulted from the institution's first recorded murder. Robert Stephens – whose name was also given as "Robert Seinous" - was attacked and stabbed by another student on July 15, 1937. Authorities arrested Leroy Taylor in connection with the crime and charged him with 1st Degree Murder. He eventually entered a plea to 2nd Degree Murder and was sentenced to state prison on November 30, 1937.[24]

University of South Florida researchers identified Stephens as a white male, but data from the 1930 census for Gadsden County shows that he was African American. He was born in around 1923 and was attending school at Quincy in 1930. Stephens ran afoul of the law for breaking and entering and was sent to the Florida Industrial School for Boys in September 1936. He had served about 10 months of a two year sentence when he was murdered.[25]

Rachel Palmer, the teenager's mother, was still living in Quincy and working as a tobacco packer at the time of his death. The records do not indicate that she retrieved his body so it is likely that he was buried at "Boot Hill." His brother, Horace, is buried at Sunnyvale Cemetery in Quincy, but there is no indication that a grave exists there for Robert.[26]

From 1900-1939, 52 graves were placed at the Dozier School Cemetery. Use of the site for new burials was nearing an end, but one of the most publicized funerals there was yet to take place.

[1] "Lee Smith, Colored Boy, Loses Life In Accident On Farm," *The Yellow Jacket*, January 16, 1932, Page 1.

[2] Florida Industrial School Ledgers, Florida State Archives; Cemetery Plat, Orange Hill Cemetery, Old Section, Garden of Peace, Tampa, Florida.

[3] *Dallas Morning News*, February 11, 1932, Section II, Page 1; *National Labor Tribune*, May 5, 1932, p. 6.

[4] "Colored Department Has Been Suffering With Epidemic of Flu," *The Yellow Jacket*, April 23, 1932, Page 1.

[5] *Ibid.*

[6] Florida Industrial School Ledgers, Florida State Archives.

[7] *Ibid.*

[8] *Ibid.*

[9] "Influenza Epidemic Proves To Be Mild," *The Yellow Jacket*, December 17, 1932, Page 1.

[10] *Ibid.*

[11] Rupert Norwood, "News of the Hospital," *The Yellow Jacket*, December 31, 1932, Page 3.

[12] *Ibid.*

[13] "Thomas Varnadoe Claimed By Death," *The Yellow Jacket*, November 3, 1934, Page 1.

[14] Ben Montgomery, "In Marianna, dig for truth encounters desire to keep past buried," *Tampa Bay Times*, April 13, 2013; "Hate Map," Southern Poverty Law Center, 2013, www.splcenter.org.

[15] Rich Philips, "Florida to exhume bodies buried at former boy school," www.cnn.com, September 2, 2013; David Usborne, "'A concentration camp for little boys': Dark secrets unearthed in KKK county," *The Guardian*, March 3, 2013.

[16] Ben Mongomery, "In Marianna, dig for truth encounters desire to keep past buried," *Tampa Bay Times*, April 13, 2013; For a history of the Neal murder, see Dale Cox, *The Claude Neal Lynching: The 1934 Murders of Claude Neal and Lola Cannady*, Old Kitchen Books, Bascom, Florida, 2014.

[17] Personal Communication, Nick Cox to the Author, April 24, 2013.

[18] Kimmerle, Interim Report, pp. 56-57 and 69.

[19] Personal Communication, Glen Varnadoe, made during discussion in basement of the Jackson County Courthouse, 2013.

[20] Press Release from USF.

[21] Florida Industrial School for Boys Ledgers, Florida State Archives.

[22] "Death Claims Grady Huff in F.I.S. Hospital," *The Yellow Jacket*, March 9, 1935.

[23] Florida Industrial School for Boys Ledgers, Florida State Archives.

[24] *Ibid.*, "Investigative Summary," Office of Executive Investigations, Florida Department of Law Enforcement, Case No. EI-73-8455, May 14, 2009, Page 15; Circuit Court Minutes for 1937, Jackson County Archives.
[25] U.S. Census for Gadsden County, Florida, 1930; Florida Industrial School Ledgers, Florida State Archives.
[26] Florida State Census for 1935; Personal inspection of Sunnyvale Cemetery, Quincy, Florida.

FOOTBALL TEAM OF 1931

DRUM AND BUGLE CORPS IN THE 1930S

EDUCATION BULDING IN THE 1930S

COTTAGES IN 1932

Seven

The Death of George Owen Smith

On Thursday, August 7, 2014, researchers from the University of South Florida (USF) announced that a body exhumed from the historic Dozier School Cemetery in Marianna, Florida, was that of George Owen Smith. The identification of Smith, a 14-year-old student who walked away from the campus in 1940, was made by researchers at the University of North Texas through the use of DNA. USF was notified of the finding on July 25 but kept the information secret until a major press conference could be scheduled and notification given to media outlets around the nation.

The announcement was followed by a predictable media explosion. Newspaper reporters and television anchors hailed the identification of Smith's remains as a "breakthrough" and "milestone" in the university's research project at Dozier School. They described the "dark" past of the institution, repeating tales of torture and murders in the dark of night. Lost in this frenzy, however, was the fact that Smith was not found at the site where a family member said that his grave was located. USF had expected to find Smith's remains in a "clandestine" second cemetery that researchers once believed was hidden somewhere on the South Campus. School records and the Florida Department of Law Enforcement indicated that the young man's grave was in the known cemetery at "Boot Hill." They were right.

This was just one of many key facts ignored by the media in its frenzied and often highly inaccurate accounting of Smith's death and burial. Here is the real story, as best it can be determined so many years after the fact.

George Owen Smith was 14-years-old when he was sentenced to the Florida Industrial School for Boys for car theft in 1940. The child of a hard-working family from Auburndale, a small city between Orlando and Tampa, Smith had been arrested in the company of an older boy after they wrecked a stolen automobile.

Given a one-year sentence by a judge in South Florida, Smith arrived in Marianna on September 20, 1940. He was described as "exceptionally friendly," but had an IQ of 73, which was considered "borderline" or "well below average." A physical examination rated his general health as only "fair."[1]

He had not been at the school long before he tried to run away. Smith's sister, Ovell Krell, told one version of the story of this first escape attempt when she wrote to authorities in Florida on April 25, 2009. Her mother had not heard from Smith in "several months" [actually 17 days], she said, and wrote to Superintendent Millard Davidson at the Boys School seeking information. "She was notified at this time that he had escaped and his whereabouts were unknown," Ms. Krell informed FDLE. "Shortly thereafter they were notified that he was in the custody of Polk County, Fl. at the sheriff's dept. in Bartow, Florida."[2]

The passage of seven decades apparently caused some understandable confusion in Ms. Krell's memories. She related to FDLE that her father went to Bartow hoping to see George but was told that the young man had already been sent back to Marianna. In reality, George Smith never left Marianna and was definitely nowhere near Polk County at the time of his first escape attempt:

...He was apprehended by a member of the school staff in Marianna about an hour after leaving, and was immediately returned to the school. For this violation of school discipline he received the usual penalty, but was restored to full privileges within three weeks and on November 9 earned an advancement....[3]

The nature of the "usual penalty" received by Smith for leaving was the subject of wild speculation by the media in 2009-2014. Ms. Krell wrote to FDLE that a former student claiming to have been present in 1940 had told her that George was taken to the building now called the "White House" and given a severe beating:

We later learned from a boy who was there at the same time that they took my brother to the White House and when they brought him out they were carrying him. The boy said they heard his screams and that he was taken to the infirmary.[4]

The White House, however, was still an ice cream factory in 1940 and did not come into use as a disciplinary facility until after World War II. As the *Jackson County Floridan* reported in 1941, the real "usual penalty" received by Smith was a "demotion" or reduction in rank.[5]

Students at the Florida Industrial School for Boys were granted privileges based on their level of rehabilitation. As they progressed through their sentence and demonstrated improvement, they moved up through a series of classifications that began with "Rookie" and ended with "Ace." Each improvement in status gave them extra privileges and benefits. Rookies and "Polliwogs," for example, were limited to lesser privileges like using library books, participating in cottage games, making purchases at the school canteen and going on supervised hikes. Aces at the other end of the scale, however, had wide ranging freedoms such as attending a weekly movie in town, writing as many letters as they wanted, having freedom of the yard until bed time and even taking leaves of absence from the school for "any reasonable lengths of time."[6]

A boy who broke the rules of the institution could expect a demotion and loss of privileges and would have to work his way back up to his former status. Corporal punishment was legal at the time and was administered by employees, especially in cases involving escape. Smith may well have received a spanking, but it would not have been in the White House at that time.

Smith regained his previous status in time to participate in a variety of campus events held for the boys on the weekend of November 9-10, 1940:

Immediately following lunch Sunday, November 10, the boys were busily engaged in a marble contest. The best seven marble shooters were selected from each cottage. Then each player was required to place five marbles in the center of a large bull-ring, thus making a total of 105 marbles in the ring.

The team which knocked out the greatest number of marbles would win a bag of candy for themselves and every boy in their cottage. Therefore each team had the enthusiastic support of their respective cottage-mates, who gave them tangible aid by supplying the members of their team with nice, new shiny "shooters."[7]

George Owen Smith was one of the seven players that represented Cottage Three in the competition, which was won by Cottage One. The shiny new "shooter" given to Smith by his cottage mates was a prize possession and may have been the one that showed up again more than 70 years later in an especially poignant way.[8]

Two weeks later on the Saturday before Thanksgiving, George Smith tried again to run away.

All students at the Florida Industrial School for Boys were assigned jobs a part of the training process. As they advanced from Pollywog to Ace, their jobs improved along with their status. George Owen Smith's first job was in the school laundry and he worked there on the morning of November 23, 1940. The students of the school were given Saturday afternoons to play and Smith spent his afternoon on the recreation yards. The playgrounds and ball fields were alive with stories of a carnival or fair underway in Marianna that week. The Aces, who enjoyed considerable freedom, had been allowed to go and they brought back tales of the rides and adventures they had experienced.

As he listened to the stories of the older students, the 14-year-old reportedly decided to run away with the carnival. He enlisted the help of another student and the two made plans to slip away from campus that night. The second student, however, turned snitch:

...Prior to leaving the school young Smith planned a joint departure with another boy, who changed his mind about leaving and tried to induce young Smith to give up the idea. This youth reported the escape plans to his cottage master and was assigned by the cottage master to try to keep watch over young Smith and try to prevent him from running away.[9]

The second youth told school officials that he was unable to convince Smith to give up his plans so the two left campus on the night of Saturday, November 23. Within an hour, however, he slipped away from George and went back to the school to alert employees:

School officials immediately started in search of Smith but were unable to pick up any clue concerning the route taken by the runaway. Learning that Smith had said he hoped to reach his uncle's home in Tampa by traveling with personnel of the fair, disbanding that night, school officials and employees of the carnival kept a close vigilance on departing vehicles but could find no trace of Smith. All main highways and railways leading out of town were also closely watched....[10]

Perhaps to hide the fact that he had "snitched" on Smith, the second boy later told a wild story of how he had been part of the escape attempt:

[H]e and my brother escaped one night and were walking towards town when they saw lights behind them and knew their absence had been discovered. The boy said he stopped and waited to be picked up but that my brother ran out across an open field. He said that the last thing he heard or saw were two or three guards shooting at my brother. I have always felt that he was shot and killed that night and had been buried to cover up the fact.[11]

The second student's role as an informer aside, there are real problems with his claims. Employment records of the Florida Industrial School for Boys at Marianna show that it did not have two or three armed guards in 1940. The school operated on an honor system and the only paid security was an unarmed night watchman.[12]

The entire story of armed guards shooting at Smith was likely a fabrication created many years after the fact. Not only had this second student not participated in the escape as he told Smith's family, he actually had alerted a cottage parent to the plan. He then abandoned a 14-year-old with an IQ of 73 in the darkness and returned to campus to sound the alarm. So far as is known, he was the last person to see George Owen Smith alive.

A heavy thunderstorm erupted over Marianna that night. The lights of employees from the school joined with those of Marianna Police officers and Jackson County Sheriff's deputies as they searched through the torrential rains for signs of the missing boy. No trace of him could be found. All that is known is that at some point that night – probably to get out of the rain or hide from authorities – George Smith somehow wound up under the home of Mrs. Ella Pierce in downtown Marianna.

MRS. ELLA PIERCE

HOME OF MRS. ELLA PIERCE

MILLARD DAVIDSON

AERIAL VIEW OF DOZIER SCHOOL FOR BOYS, SHOWING WHERE MRS. KRELL THOUGHT GEORGE OWEN SMITH WAS BURIED (A) AND WHERE HIS GRAVE WAS ACTUALLY FOUND (B) IN THE KNOWN DOZIER SCHOOL CEMETERY. THE TWO POINTS ARE ROUGHLY ONE-MILE APART.

Mrs. Pierce lived near Marianna City Hall at the corner of Market and Green Streets. She neither saw nor heard anything unusual that night. In fact, two months would pass before an unseasonable heat wave led to the discovery of Smith's body.

The search for George Owen Smith continued for more than two months after he walked away from the campus on the night of November 23, 1940. Concern for his well-being grew among both his family and the school staff as no trace of the youth could be found. That the school did notify the Smith family of George's second disappearance is evident from the wording of a letter from Superintendent Millard Davidson to Mrs. Smith on January 1, 1941:

This is to acknowledge receipt of your letter of recent date written with regard to your son, George Owen, and to advise that so far we have been unable to get any information concerning his whereabouts...We will be glad to get in touch with you just as soon as we are able to locate George and in the meantime we will appreciate your notifying us immediately if you receive any word from or concerning him.[13]

The letter makes no mention of George's escape, a clear indication that the superintendent and Mrs. Smith had already communicated about his disappearance. Otherwise Davidson would have offered a more detailed explanation. His use of the words "so far" in telling Mrs. Smith that the school had been unable to learn anything about the youth's whereabouts also indicates that the two had communicated previously about George's disappearance.

The mystery of George Owen Smith's whereabouts came to an end on the morning of January 24, 1941:

Odors which had been faintly observed at first by the members of the Pierce household gradually became more pronounced and caused a search to be made which led to the discovery of the boy's body under the house. It was discovered by Levi Rivers...employed by the city of Marianna, who at the direction of local officers placed the body on a blanket, using electrician's rubber gloves and moved it from under the house into the yard.[14]

Members of the Pierce family recall today that the body was actually found by the family's gardener. He crawled under the house along with a 5-year old member of the Pierce family. It was an experience the young boy never forgot and discussed with others until he passed away in 1999. Family members today believe that George was definitely still alive when he crawled under the house:

...They found it huddled next to the kitchen chimney which was lit 24/7. [Five] chimneys on that house hit the ground and Owen curled up next to the warmest. This was why my great-grandfather thought he was alive in November crawling under the house. He also examined the body after it was pulled into the yard. There was never any discussion about him being shot, ever.[15]

The great-grandfather mentioned in the above account was a physician. The family member recalled that the death was never discussed by those living in the house as anything other than a sad tragedy.[16]

That the body had been under the house for a significant length of time was evident from the fact that it was severely decayed. George's face was no longer recognizable, but police officers recognized the rotting clothing as being of the type worn by students at the Florida Industrial School. Superintendent Davidson was notified and immediately came to the scene, bringing with him future superintendent Arthur G. Dozier and another employee.[17]

Mr. Dozier examined the body and determined that although it was decomposed beyond recognition, locks of scattered hair found with it were similar to those of George Owen Smith. Laundry marks were also found on the body's clothing consistent with those used at the school. Mr. Dozier had [Levi Rivers] turn back the clothing to look for the laundry mark, which was verified by an immediate call to the school office as being the one assigned to George Smith.[18]

Superintendent Davidson examined the body as well and then discussed the gruesome discovery with Sheriff Barkley Gause and County Judge D.H. Oswald. Gause did not believe that any meaningful evidence could be obtained from the severely decomposed body, but Davidson insisted that a Coroner's inquest be held. Visibly shaken, he felt that such a measure was necessary to "positively identify the body and get a legally and logically acceptable explanation of the tragedy if possible."[19]

Modern media claims that no investigation took place are completely false. The Coroner's Jury was empaneled and after its members had viewed the body was dismissed until the following morning. Sheriff Gause assigned a deputy to guard Smith's remains until arrangements could be made for burial. The members of the Jackson County Coroner's Jury met the next morning, reviewed all of the available evidence and immediately returned a verdict that George Owen Smith had died from an unknown cause.[20]

Numerous media outlets have insinuated that Smith's family was not notified of his death prior to his burial. This also is false:

A call was made by Superintendent Davidson to the Reverend J. Erwin Wherry, Presbyterian minister of Auburndale, requesting him to convey news of the boy's death to his parents and to ascertain their wishes. The parents, it was learned, did not at first consent for the body to be buried here, but insisted that it be returned by the school to Auburndale.[21]

In her 2009 letter to FDLE, Ms. Krell remembered that her family communicated with a funeral home. This is confirmed by the January 31, 1941, issue of the *Jackson County Floridan*:

Morticians here and in Auburndale, however, advised that the body be buried immediately, as the expense of preparing it for a delayed burial or for transporting it to Auburndale would amount to at least $500. After conferring with state officials, it was decided to make interment here and Ven. V.G. Lowery, rector of St. Luke's Episcopal Church, was called to officiate at the simple ceremony which was held at the graveside at 3:30 o'clock Friday afternoon. Present were members of the school staff, the representative of the sheriff's office, and the boys who assisted at the grave.[22]

The graveside funeral at the Dozier School Cemetery was also covered by student writers for The *Yellow Jacket*, the school's newspaper. These accounts refute media claims that Smith was dumped in a "shallow hole." So too does a letter written by the minister that conducted the services:

Being Mr. Davidson's Pastor, and also having a fairly good knowledge of the School and the fine work they are doing for so many of the boys in our State,

I readily agreed to conduct a burial service for George. At about 3:30 o'clock Friday afternoon, the 24th, I conducted the burial service for George, in the presence of Mr. Davidson and members of the staff. It was in the Burial Plot of the School, that is kept nicely cleaned and cared for, and will be looked after in the years to come. So please know your son's last rites were tenderly and considerately performed.[23]

Rev. Lowery also noted that Superintendent Davidson had been greatly disturbed by the boy's tragic death. "[W]hile he was waiting for your local Presbyterian Minister to talk with you and Mr. Smith about this tragedy and report back to him," Lowery wrote, "he called me out to the School, told me how troubled he was about this untimely end to George's life, how sorry he felt for you all, and that he wouldn't have had it happen for anything."[24]

Lowery's letter confirms the *Jackson County Floridan* report that local authorities investigated the death:

...All sorts of investigations were carried on, and all day [Davidson] kept trying to figure out just how it could have happened. Every now and then he would refer to George's parents and how hard a blow it must be to you all. His kindest thoughts and concern have certainly been for you in the loss of your boy.[25]

Although the body was severely decomposed making such examinations difficult at best, neither police officers nor the members of the Coroner's Jury could find any visible wounds. Even after he was given approval to proceed with burying the body, Superintendent Davidson insisted that one more attempt be made. An autopsy was conducted:

Although assured by both the mortician and the doctor that an autopsy would be useless if not impossible, Superintendent Davidson and Dr. C.D. Whittaker in the presence of the deputy sheriff and other witnesses, conducted a final examination of the body before burial and were able to positively identify it by dental structure which when compared with school records showed it to be that of George Owen Smith.[26]

Although the surviving documentation indicates they had given their permission for the school to bury the 14-year-old in its cemetery, George's parents made arrangements to visit Marianna. Records indicate that they arrived on Sunday, January 26, two days after Smith's body was discovered. Mrs. Krell over the years appears to have become slightly confused about the date, telling the media that the family visited on the day after George's body was found (i.e. January 25).

Her statement that a letter from Rev. Lowery was waiting the next day when they returned home, however, verifies that the visit was on the 26th and that the family arrived back home on the 27th, a Monday. Then as now, there was no mail delivery on Sundays.

Mrs. Krell's own words indicate there was no effort on the part of school employees to hide the grave:

...We were shown a fresh pile of dirt in a cemetery and were told that was where my brother was buried. Unfortunately, my parents did not have the means to have the body excavated and moved to our home town, so we had to leave him buried there.[27]

The family never returned to place a permanent marker on George's grave and, as best as can be determined, never visited the cemetery again.

The University of South Florida made clear that one of the objectives of its science project at Dozier School for Boys was to determine what happened to George Owen Smith. This goal was spurred on in part by media reports, some of which quoted Mrs. Krell as saying she believed that school authorities shot Smith, buried him, dug him back up, moved him up to town, hid the body under Mrs. Pierce's house so he would be discovered, then moved him back to campus and finally buried him again.[28]

Ms. Krell pointed out a site on the South campus not far from the administration building as the place where her brother was buried. The location identified by her is on the opposite side of Highway 167 and roughly one mile from the known Dozier School Cemetery. Former students even verified her claim, telling USF researchers that they had seen graves at the same spot.

The researchers were convinced, stating conclusively in their interim report not only that there was a second cemetery in the location indicated by Mrs.

Krell, but that the known cemetery contained only the remains of African American students. "In 1941, Superintendent Davidson personally showed the Smith family a grave on the South side or white school," they wrote, "thereby demonstrating that the burials were not integrated and that multiple burial locations existed."[29]

USF researchers did not realize it at the time, but they had already found George Owen Smith. His was the very first grave exhumed at the known or "Boot Hill" Cemetery, a body initially reported to be that of a young African American student. Not only was the body not African American, despite claims by researchers, a U.S. Senator and the media that the "Boot Hill" cemetery contained only the remains of black students, but it was found exactly where the Florida Department of Law Enforcement (FDLE) and Dozier School said it had been buried. There was no cemetery at the location pointed out by Mrs. Krell and former students.

This latter bit of information in a report filed by the university with the office of State Archaeologist Dr. Mary Glowacki. The media was not alerted to the filing and USF officials made clear efforts to downplay their failure to find any trace of the rumored "second cemetery." Dr. Elizabeth Bird, the overall head of the university's Department of Anthropology, responded in this manner to one concerned citizen who wrote to ask about the report:

As far as I know, there is nothing new to report. The team is busy this summer, mostly doing analysis, and I'm sure there will be announcements when appropriate.[30]

Ben Montgomery, the *Tampa Bay Times* reporter, took a similar stance, telling the same individual that "there's nothing newsworthy in this." Employees at WJHG-TV in Panama City, Florida, even questioned whether the report really existed until a copy was provided to them by this author. A few stories followed, but they were limited to stations WJHG and WMBB in Panama City and the *Jackson County Floridan* and *Jackson County Times* in Marianna. The statewide and national media ignored the news, which would turn out to be much more "newsworthy" than any of them realized.[31]

Senator Nelson's office, however, was growing concerned. On July 15, 2014, one of his staff members wrote to USF's project leader questioning an "odd message" about the South Campus report. Dr. Erin Kimmerle responded that "some folks misrepresented what that meant/means for our work."[32]

The truth finally hit USF researchers in the face on July 25, 2014, when the DNA lab at the University of North Texas notified them that the very first body they had exhumed in 2013 was, in fact, George Owen Smith. USF employees notified Ms. Krell that her brother's remains had been identified, but otherwise maintained silence on the matter for two more weeks. During that time they notified media across the country that they would be making a major announcement on August 8, 2014.[33]

The announcement, of course, was that the body of George Owen Smith had been identified. The media went wild. USF's unequivocal statements that the "multiple burial locations existed" and that the graves in the known "Boot Hill" Cemetery "were not integrated" were ignored, as were the media's own claims that "early lab work suggests existence of second Dozier cemetery."[34]

The media also glossed over USF's admission that it was unable to determine a cause of death for George Owen Smith. The university's anthropologists not only had been unable to determine that the body was that of a white individual, but reached a conclusion that was exactly the same as the one reached by the Jackson County Coroner's Jury some 73 years before.

The media did come up with some new false statements to replace old false statements. Jared Leone and Terry Spencer wrote for the *Tallahassee Democrat*, for example, that some of the bodies exhumed by USF "were found under roads or overgrown trees, well away from the white, metal crosses" in the memorial area at the "Boot Hill" cemetery. This claim of bodies being found under roads was picked up by wire services and repeated by media outlets all over the country.[35]

No bodies were found under area roads. USF itself reported that an exploratory trench excavated in the "historical road that provided access to the site" had "failed to identify any evidence of grave shafts or possible grave shafts.[36]

A wire service report went so far as to claim that Smith's body had not been buried in a coffin, but instead had simply been wrapped in a shroud and tossed in a hole. *Tampa Bay Times* writer Ben Montgomery, however, had already reported that coffin hardware was found in association with the body. Montgomery, who was allowed special access to the dig site in 2013 even as local reporters were denied the opportunity to cover the work first-hand, reported of the first body that it had been found in association with coffin handles. He did not know at that time, of course, that he was seeing the remains of George Owen Smith.[37]

Dr. Kimmerle confirmed in the same story that the body had been buried in a coffin, telling Montgomery that "hardware" had been found. She dated the grave to the era of the 1940s. The "hardware" consisted of handles, nails, screws and other items used in the manufacture of coffins.[38]

The grave of George Owen Smith is also believed to be the one from which researchers found a marble, possibly the "shooter" given to him by the other boys of his cottage two weeks before he vanished from the school. It adds a necessary reminder of the humanity of the young boy buried in the grave.

In the end it is obvious that the nation was subjected to an impressive list of inaccuracies and falsehoods about the death and burial of George Owen Smith. The new findings by USF and the University of North Texas are, in fact, identical to the conclusions reached by the Jackson County Coroner's Jury more than 70 years ago. Thanks to the University of North Texas, we also know that George Owen Smith had already been found even as USF continued searching for him one mile away from the place where FDLE correctly reported that he was buried.

Why George Owen Smith's family did not visit often enough to remember the location of the grave and why they did not permanently mark the burial place of their son is not known.

So what did happen to George Owen Smith? School employees in 1941 speculated that he might have died of pneumonia after crawling under Mrs. Pierce's house. That is certainly a possibility. Members of the Pierce family found Smith's body curled up next to the kitchen fireplace and assumed that he had done so in an effort to stay warm. Cold and wet, he certainly would have been suffering from exposure. Beyond that all that can truthfully be said is that the young man's death was a tragedy. He now rests alongside his family and hopefully does so in peace.

[1] *Jackson County Floridan*, January 31, 1941.

[2] Ovell Smith Krell to Florida Department of Law Enforcement, April 25, 2009 (hereafter Krell to FDLE, 2009).

[3] *Jackson County Floridan*, January 31, 1941.

[4] Krell to FDLE, 2009.

[5] *Jackson County Floridan*, January 31, 1941.

[6] "Information Booklet on the Rating System of the Florida Industrial School for Boys," February 10, 1936.

[7] "Marble Shooting," *The Yellow Jacket*, November 23, 1940, Page 2.

[8] *Ibid.*

[9] *Jackson County Floridan*, January 31, 1941.

[10] *Ibid.*

[11] Krell to FDLE, 2009.

[12] "Faculty Members – White Department," Florida Industrial School for Boys, July 1, 1940.

[13] Millard Davidson, Superintendent, to Mrs. Smith, January 1, 1941.

[14] *Jackson County Floridan*, January 31, 1941.

[15] Personal Communication from Pierce family member (name withheld by author), August 13, 2014.

[16] *Ibid.*

[17] *Jackson County Floridan*, January 31, 1941.

[18] *Ibid.*

[19] *Ibid.*

[20] *Ibid.*

[21] *Ibid.*

[22] *Ibid.*

[23] Rev. V.G. Lowery to Mrs. George W. Smith, January 25, 1941.

[24] *Ibid.*

[25] *Ibid.*

[26] *Jackson County Floridan*, January 31, 1941.

[27] Krell to FDLE, 2009.

[28] Reported by numerous media websites.

[29] Kimmerle EH, Estabrook R, Wells EC, Jackson AT. 2012. Documentation of the Boot Hill Cemetery (8JA1860) at the former Arthur G. Dozier School for Boys, Interim Report, Division of Historical Resources Permit No. 1112.032, December 10, 2012 (hereafter USF Interim Report), p. 56.

[30] Dr. Elizabeth Byrd to [name withheld by request], July 11, 2014.

[31] Ben Montgomery to [name withheld by request], July 13, 2014; Personal conversation with WJHG staff.

[32] Susie PerezQuinn to Dr. Erin Kimmerle, July 15, 2014; Dr. Erin Kimmerle to Susie PerezQuinn, July 15, 2014, (Emails obtained using Florida's Open Records statutes).

[33] Emails obtained from USF's media relations office using Florida's Sunshine Law and Open Records statutes.

[34] Ben Montgomery (Insert Nelson Second Cemetery Reference)

[35] *Tallahassee Democrat*, August 8, 2014.

[36] USF Interim Report, p. 34.

[37] Ben Montgomery, "First remains from Dozier graves identified as 14-year-old boy," *Tampa Bay Times*, August 8, 2014.

[38] *Ibid.*

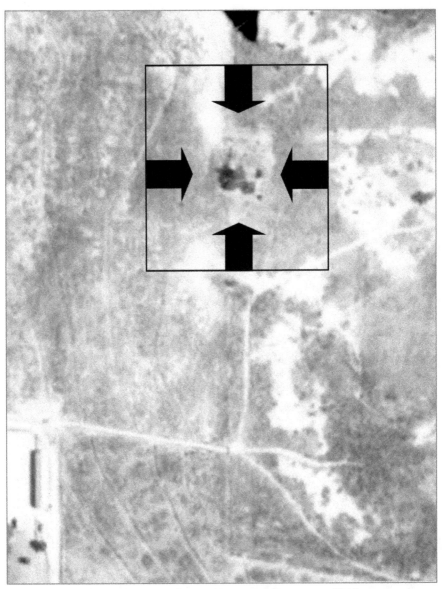

DOZIER SCHOOL CEMETERY FROM THE AIR IN 1940.

Eight

Last Burials at "Boot Hill"

THE LAST KNOWN BURIALS AT THE DOZIER SCHOOL CEMETERY took place in 1944 and 1952. Other deaths occurred in 1941-1973, but the remains were buried in off campus cemeteries. A tabulation of those burial sites will follow at the end of this chapter.

Earl Wilson was the only student in the history of the school known to have died while confined for disciplinary purposes. His death, however, was not associated with the structure known today as the "White House."

Wilson 12 years old when he was confined with seven other students in a building known as "the shed" on the North or "colored" campus of Florida Industrial School for Boys. The structure was a tiny 70 square foot building with a tin roof and conditions for the students confined there, who ranged in age from 11 to 17, can only be described as abysmal. It was late August and temperatures were above normal as was the humidity.[1]

The eight African American students in the "shed" each had a space of less than 3-feet by 3-feet in which to survive. Ventilation was limited as was lighting. The door was padlocked from the outside and the students had one bucket for drinking water and a second bucket to use as a toilet. The latter container was emptied only once per day. There can be no doubt that the conditions in which the employees of the North campus – most of them also African American – placed the eight young black students would be considered torture today.[2]

In this situation at least four of the detainees began to at least discuss the possibility of making their escape. These four – Charles Bevels, Robert Farmer, Floyd Alexander and William Foxworth – allegedly became convinced that Earl

Wilson planned to inform school employees of their breakout plan. By the morning of September 1, 1944, he was dead. Foxworth, Alexander, Bevels and Farmer were arrested and charged with murder. The other four youths in the "shed" when the killing happened were called as prosecution witnesses:

At the trial, which lasted one day, the prosecution's theory was that the four defendants had choked Earl Wilson by holding him down and pressing a stick against his throat. The theory was presented in the versions of the facts related by the four boys who testified for the prosecution. These witnesses also testified that earlier in the day one of the defendants, Charles Bevels, had struck Earl Wilson repeatedly with the stick.[3]

Dr. C.D. Whittaker, the school physician, examined Wilson's body and conducted an autopsy:

...The medical evidence, given by a doctor summoned when Earl Wilson was found dead, was that death was caused by blows to the head with a blunt instrument. A dissection of the decedent's neck muscles revealed no bruises.[4]

Defense attorneys offered an alternate theory that the four eyewitnesses in the case were actually the murderers. The jury, however, did not believe the alternate version offered of the murder and convicted Bevels, Farmer, Alexander and Wainwright of murder:

Four Negro youths yesterday were found guilty here of first degree murder in the slaying of another Negro, Earl Wilson, 14. The jury recommended mercy.

The slaying occurred on August 31 at the Florida Industrial School for Boys, at Marianna, all of the principals being inmates of the institution. Wilson's body was found early on the morning of that day by attendants in a room where the five had been confined for disciplinary purposes. He had been bludgeoned to death, evidence disclosed.

The four convicted are Charles Bevels, 17, Robert Farmer, 17, William Foxworth, 14, and Floyd Alexander, 18.[5]

The four avoided the death penalty when they were sentenced to life in prison. Their case was appealed to the Florida Supreme Court but the justices affirmed the sentence.[6]

William Foxworth appealed to the 5th Circuit U.S. Court of Appeals some 30 years later after being denied relief by the U.S. District Court. The claim asserted in his appeal was that he had been denied effective legal counsel because he was represented by the same attorney as Charles Bevels, with whom he had a major conflict of interest. In essence, Foxworth alleged that Bevels alone was responsible for the murder of Earl Wilson but that he (Foxworth) had been unable to assert this during his original trial because his attorney also represented Bevels:

In this case an actual, substantial conflict of interest emerged early in the trial. The first witness was a physician, who testified that Earl Wilson's death was caused by blows to the top of the head with a blunt instrument. The second witness for the prosecution was Curtis Wilson, one of the other boys in the cell when the murder occurred. Although his answers were not too clear, the thrust of his testimony was that Charles Bevels had beaten decedent badly on the head with a stick shortly before their supper was brought to the cell. After supper, he testified, Bevels pressed the stick to the decedent's neck while the other three defendants held him down, thus choking him. Thus if the medical testimony was correct and the prosecution's first eyewitness was to be believed, Bevels alone participated in the death-dealing blows. Foxworth was implicated only in part of the sequence of events that, according to the doctor, was not the cause of death.[7]

The court ruled in favor of Foxworth in 1975, reversing an earlier decision of the U.S. District Court for the Northern District of Florida. His conviction was set aside and after spending more than 30 years behind bars for murder, the man was ordered released from prison.

Earl Wilson was buried at the Dozier School Cemetery on September 1 or 2, 1944. His interment was the next to last to take place at "Boot Hill."

The next death to take place at the school was also a murder. Eddie Albert Black, 13, was beaten, strangled and stabbed by another student on May 4, 1949:

Young Black's body was found in the culvert by another Industrial School boy after he had been missing half an hour from the school laundry where he had been working. The culvert runs beneath the highway which divides the white and colored sides of the school, and the body was found some distance from the opening. It was lying face down on the concrete floor of the culvert, which is used as a drain from the school laundry, but usually does not carry enough water to cause drowning.[8]

Dr. C.D. Whittaker was called to the scene, as were officers from the Marianna Police Department and Jackson County Sheriff's Office. The Marianna Fire Department also came and used a respirator in an attempt to revive Black but he could not be saved. That the youth had died from foul play was evident and a coroner's jury was convened by Justice of the Peace E.C. Davis.[9]

The autopsy conducted by Dr. Whittaker revealed that the "cuts about the throat and head" were superficial, but that the student had been strangled and received a brain injury. A joint investigation was launched by Marianna Police officers and Jackson County Sheriff's deputies, but as they began their work two suspects were quickly identified by school administrators:

On Thursday morning, when the coroner's inquest was scheduled to be continued, it was learned that Frank Odell Murphy, Jr., 14, of Lakeland, had confessed to the actual slaying of young Black, and implicated Abelardo Quevedo, 17, of Tampa. Murphy was serving a sentence for grand larceny, while Quevedo had been sent up on conviction of armed robbery. The confession of murphy was made to Superintendent Arthur Dozier, who brought the boys to the court house for a hearing on the charge.

Abelardo Quevedo told State Attorney Mercer P. Spear that Murphy told him in advance of a plan to kill Eddie Black. According to news leaked to the *Jackson County Floridan* newspaper, Quevedo confirmed "that Murphy had told him on one occasion that he had often had the desire to kill someone."[10]

The story as told by Murphy was related by Superintendent Dozier, for whom the school was later named:

The Murphy boy told Superintendent Dozier that he had lured young Black into the culvert and beaten him to death. His only reason was that Black had caught him smoking, and that he feared he would report him. He also used a knife, which he said was loaned him by Quevedo, and that Quevedo had "offered to help him do the job." He refused, he said, "because I was afraid if we both went, we'd be missed."[11]

The matter was referred to the Jackson County Grand Jury which returned True Bills against Murphy and Quevedo. Frank Murphy was indicted for 1st Degree Murder while Abelardo Quevedo was indicted for Accessory to 1st Degree Murder.[12]

The two went to trial before Circuit Judge E.C. Welch on June 2, 1949. By that time the murder was being described as a "tattle tale" killing. Superintendent Dozier testified that Murphy told him that the killing took place after Eddie Black saw him smoking and called out, "Oh, ho, I am going to have to see what I can do about that." Jackson County Sheriff Earnest Barnes testified that Murphy had "borrowed a pen knife from Quevedo to use on Black."[13]

The two were convicted and sentenced to prison, Murphy for 2nd Degree Murder after he entered a plea and Quevedo for Accessory to Murder. More than two decades later, however, Frank Murphy appealed his conviction. In this appeal he told a different story about what had happened:

> ...His position now is that he engaged in a fist fight with the decedent and nothing more. The fight stopped when both were exhausted. Decedent was found shortly thereafter at the scene of the fight dead of knife wounds. Appellant contends that he received a note from a fellow inmate while in jail awaiting trial advising him that there were three witnesses who saw decedent leave the scene of the fight just after appellant. Apparently the decedent then returned to the scene to look for something.[14]

Frank Murphy's claim before the U.S. Court of Appeals, in essence, was that he did not kill Eddie Black. The filing asserted that Murphy and Black had been involved in a fistfight but that some unidentified person stabbed Black to death a short time later. This was counter to the findings of Dr. Whittaker that the stab wounds suffered by Murphy had been superficial and that he had actually died from being strangled and beaten.

Murphy's attorneys alleged that the prosecutor knew of the mysterious note passed to the youth while he was in jail and was trying to determine its validity. Sheriff Earnest Barnes was also aware of the note and supposedly questioned Black about it:

> ...During a recess the sheriff interrogated appellant in an effort to learn how he managed to receive the note in jail. The sheriff is said to have made certain threats regarding the horror of dying in the electric chair and advised appellant that it would be the part of wisdom to enter a plea to second degree murder....[15]

While the intervention of Sheriff Barnes with Murphy was portrayed in a sinister way in the appeal, his intent could well have been to save the youth from death in the electric chair. Coverage of the murders of both Eddie Black and Earl

Wilson at the Florida Industrial School for Boys noted concern on the part of authorities that the suspects in each might face the electric chair if convicted of 1st Degree Murder. Efforts that are well-intentioned can easily be made to appear otherwise in legal filings. In the case of Frank Murphy, the alleged intervention by the Jackson County Sheriff was given the appearance of being an effort to coerce a confession.[16]

The Fifth Circuit U.S. Court of Appeals agreed with the characterization that Murphy had been coerced to confess. His conviction was vacated and he was ordered released from prison.[17]

Eddie Black, the victim of the crime, was returned home for burial by Maddox-Backburn Funeral Home.

The last person known to have been buried in the "Boot Hill" cemetery was a young African American student named Billey Jackson. He died from pyelonephritis on October 7, 1952. Some former students, however, claimed that he had been beaten prior to his death by employees of the school.[18]

The Florida Department of Law Enforcement (FDLE) reviewed these and other claims in 2012 after Governor Charlie Crist ordered an investigation of the Dozier School Cemetery:

The news media has interviewed some of these former students and included their accounts in articles regarding this investigation. One such incident includes a student who was interviewed by the media and stated that in 1953, he was asked to help dig the grave of a fellow student named "Billy." The student stated that the last time he saw "Billy" his stomach was bloated. The student stated that "Billy" died two weeks later and was buried in the School's cemetery. FDLE obtained records that identified "Billy" has Billey Jackson of Daytona Beach, who according to his death certificate, died on October 7, 1952, at the Jackson County Hospital of pyelonephritis (kidney infection) due to hydro-nephrosis (obstruction). According to the death certificate, the interval between symptom onset and death was ten days.[19]

FDLE's determination was that Billey Jackson had died from natural causes, not from a beating by school employees. The medical records show that he received treatment for 10 days prior to his death.

The University of South Florida (USF) raised questions about this conclusion, noting that two former students claimed that Jackson had been beaten before his death because he had run away from the school. One of the former students repeated

92

school rumor that Jackson had been missing prior to his funeral, an absence likely explained by the fact that he was receiving treatment at Jackson Hospital.[20]

USF lead researcher Erin Kimmerle requested that Dr. Laura Hair and Dr. Leszek Chrostowski of the District 13 Medical Examiner Department in Tampa review Jackson's death and offer their expert opinion. Why the researcher did not request an opinion from Dr. Michael Hunter, the Medical Examiner of the 14th Judicial Circuit where Billey Jackson actually died and was buried, is not known.

The two associated medical examiners from Tampa explained that pyelonephritis is a urinary tract infection and could result from an inadequate valve mechanism or obstruction. Their conclusion was that despite the allegations of a beating, it was possible that Jackson could have died a natural death. Since USF's researchers could not find a copy of the original autopsy performed by Dr. Whittaker, the two doctors could not reach a final determination from the information provided to them. They informed Kimmerle on October 18, 2012, that the cause of death for Jackson remained unknown to them.[21]

The determination from the original autopsy conducted in 1952 was that Jackson died from a kidney infection caused by an obstruction. He was buried at "Boot Hill" following a funeral presided over by a minister.

Billey Jackson was the last person known to have been buried at the Dozier School Cemetery.

Several deaths involving students from took place over the following two decades, but the death rate at the school dropped drastically during the second half of the Twentieth Century. Clarence Cunningham died from a Mestastasis to his spinal cord at W.T. Edwards Hospital in Tampa in 1954 and was buried away from the school. George Fordom, Jr., died at W.T. Edwards from lung sarcoma in January 1957 and also was buried away from the school.[22]

Edgar Thomas Elton died while playing basketball on July 10, 1961. An autopsy determined that the cause of his death was "acute dilation of heart." He was returned home and is buried at Umatilla Cemetery in Lake County, Florida.[23]

Robert Jerald Hewett died from gunshot wounds to the chest after running away from the school on April 2, 1960. He was located at his home near Cypress two days later and died from a single shotgun blast. When authorities went into the house, Hewett was found deceased with a 12-gauge shotgun near his body. Deputies from the Jackson County Sheriff's Department investigated and concluded that his wounds were self-inflicted. Some family members believe, however, that he was murdered and the University of South Florida has proposed exhuming his body. He is buried at Cypress Baptist Church Cemetery. As of the publication date of this volume, no exhumation had taken place.[24]

The only student known to have been killed by an authority in the history of the Boys School was Raymond Alex Phillips, who escaped with a second student in September 1961. The two allegedly stole a car but were spotted in Gainesville by an Alachua County Sheriff's Deputy. The second escapee surrendered when confronted by the deputy, but Phillips attempts to flee. The officer fired two warning shots over his head in an effort to get him to stop. Phillips continued to run and the officer fired what he indicated was a third warning shot, but the bullet struck Phillips in the back of the head and killed him. He is buried at Antioch Cemetery in the Island Grove community of Alachua County.[25]

Another escapee, James Lee Fredere, died on May 10, 1965. He had traveled as far as Volusia County before he was killed in an automobile accident. He is buried at Garden of Memories Cemetery in Bladen County, North Carolina.[26]

The last reported death on campus was that of Alphonse or Alphonso Glover who drowned in the swimming pool on August 13, 1966. The University of South Florida researchers were unable to find information on Glover, claiming in their interim report that the "cause and manner of his death are unknown." USF, however, flatly refused an opportunity to review thousands of pages of documents on deaths at Dozier School for Boys. Among the reports that the researchers declined to review was the report of the Jackson County Coroner on the death of Alphonso Glover.[27]

According to that report, filed by County Judge and Coroner Julian Laramore on August 15, 1966, the school notified the county sheriff on the afternoon of August 13, 1966, that there had been a drowning at the Florida School for Boys. Laramore proceeded to the campus where he interviewed James N. Smith, Glover's cottage parent:

...He stated that he was aware that the deceased, Alphonso Glover, went up on the diving board and saw him dive into the water; that he observed him as he came to the surface and that he went back down – apparently, swimming under water; that he did not hear Glover yell for help or indicate that he was in distress. He stated that a few moments later he was informed by one of the other students that someone was on the bottom of the pool; that he himself immediately dived into the pool in an effort to rescue the body from the bottom of the pool and that the first time he was unable to make it and had to resurface for additional air. On the second attempt he brought the body to the surface.[28]

Mr. Smith said that he immediately began administering artificial respiration to Glover while he waited for an ambulance to arrive from the school hospital. Personnel from the hospital soon arrived and also tried to revive Glover, but without success.[29]

A number of students were witnesses to the drowning, among them the youth assigned to be the "buddy" of Glover under the school's buddy system:

...He stated that the "buddy" system is a system whereby two boys are assigned as buddies and they are to keep an eye on each other and keep in contact with each other when they are in the pool swimming. He stated that he was in the shallow end of the pool and that he did not see anything; in fact he said he was unaware of the fact that his buddy, Alphonso Glover, had departed from the shallow end of the pool and had gone to the deep end of the pool to dive from the diving board.[30]

Two other students did see Glover go off the diving board at the deep end of the pool and one indicated that there had been a problem:

...He stated that Glover dived off the diving board; that he apparently slipped when he ran out on the end of the diving board, but that his head definitely did not hit the board or either side of the pool – that he went off the board and hit the water head first.[31]

Glover's body had been taken to the hospital by ambulance but when efforts to revive him failed, it was turned over to People's Funeral Home in Marianna. After completing his interviews with eyewitnesses, Laramore went to the funeral home to examine the body. The examination revealed no broken bones, marks or lacerations except for a small "laceration or skinned area on the right check." He concluded that this mark apparently came about as a result of Glover's face scraping the bottom of the pool or "when he was pulled along poolside by Mr. Smith and the boys for the purpose of administering artificial respiration.[32]

Contrary to the statement by USF that the "cause and manner" of Glover's death were unknown, Laramore entered a ruling on the student's death:

...After considering all the testimony and the evidence adduced in this matter, it is therefore ordered and adjudged that Alphonso Glover, colored male date of birth 9-10-52, a student at the Florida School for Boys in Marianna, Florida, came to his death at approximately 4:15 P.M. on August 13, 1966 by accidental drowning.[33]

As noted above, Glover's remains were turned over to People's Funeral Home in Marianna for arrangements.

The last death associated with Dozier School for Boys took place on April 28, 1973. Employees had taken a group for a chaperoned canoe outing on the Chipola River when a snake was spotted. One of the students, Martin E. Williams, was terrified of snakes and in a moment of panic tipped a canoe and fell into the river. A second student also fell into the water. Students and employees immediately tried to rescue the two and the second student was saved but Williams drowned before he could be pulled from the river. His remains were returned home to Hillsborough County where he is buried at Rest Haven Memorial Park Cemetery.

Several employees present at the time of Williams' accidental drowning still live in the Marianna area and remember the event with great sadness.

Researchers from the University of South Florida included one additional death in their 2012 interim report that has not been mentioned in this chapter. Michael Smelley, 16, died on March 15, 1966 from carcinoma of his spine and lungs. Citing a 2009 media report by Ben Montgomery of the *St. Petersburg Times* (AKA *Tampa Bay Times*), the USF team reported that witnesses had claimed that Smelley tried to escape and was severely beaten by employees of the school. He was unable to walk following this beating, according to the claims, and within just a few days was admitted to the prison hospital at Raiford and later transferred to the medical center at the University of Florida.[34]

The university went so far as to submit information on Smelley's death to forensic pathologists in Tampa for review to determine if the beating the young man allegedly received on the Dozier campus could have caused his spinal tumor to spread leading to an early death. USF did not explain why it did not submit this information to the Medical Examiner in Okaloosa County where Smelley actually died.[35]

The two pathologists – Dr. Laura Hair and Dr. Leszek Chrostowski – determined that Smelley died a "natural death" and that his body showed no signs of trauma. Based on their review of the records associated with Smelley's death, the doctors concluded that "if a beating occurred, it cannot be linked with this person's death." The doctors also noted that any attempt to connect a beating with the spread of a spinal neoplasm was "not likely and very speculative" in the first place.[36]

The medical evidence wasn't the only problem with the claims about Michael Smelley's death. USF noted that its researchers did not have access to state files about the teenager's incarceration but did not state whether the team filed a petition with a circuit judge to have his records opened. This is the normal process for obtaining access to juvenile records for research purposes.[37]

The Florida Department of Law Enforcement, however, did have access to the young man's records. In a statement issued on December 18, 2012, FDLE reported that it did not consider Smelley's death to be associated with Dozier School "due to the fact that he was no longer a student and had been transferred to Raiford Prison over two (2) years prior to his death."[38]

The fact that Smelley was transferred from the school to Raiford two years before he died explains why he was taken to the hospital or infirmary there instead of the one on campus. It also explains why, following his treatment at the University of Florida, the young man was returned to Raiford instead of the Boys School at Marianna.

The USF researchers failed to mention that Michael Smelley actually died at home in Okaloosa County. Montgomery did at least pick up on this fact in his original report, noting that Smelley was released from Raiford to the care of his mother prior to his death. The article reported that he died just before his 17th birthday and was buried in an unmarked grave at a Baptist church cemetery in Crestview.[39]

FDLE's conclusion that Smelley's death was not associated with the school stands for itself. A total of 11 students died at what became Dozier School for Boys in 1942-1973. Two of these were murdered by other students, four died from medical problems, two drowned, one was killed in an automobile accident, on was shot by a deputy in Alachua County and one died from what law enforcement officers ruled to be an apparent suicide.

Two of these individuals were buried in the school cemetery on "Boot Hill." The graves for Earl Wilson and Billey Jackson were the last known interments in the cemetery, which has not been used for human burials since 1952.

A 1947 issue of the *Yellow Jacket* verifies that students of the school held "an elaborate funeral service" at the cemetery that year for their pet peacock. The peacock was named "Sue" and was popular with the students. "She lies on 'Boot Hill," the article noted, "beside the bodies of several other of Marianna's deceased." Other sources indicate that several pet dogs were also buried in the cemetery vicinity.[40]

1973 brought the history of death at Dozier School to an end. From the opening of the school until the death of Martin Williams in 1973, records indicate that 101 people died at or in association with the school. The following chart lists those who died in 1942-1973:

Name	Date	Cause of Death	Burial Location
Earl Wilson	8/31/1944	Murdered by 4 students	School Cemetery
Eddie Black	5/1949	Murdered by a student	Santa Rosa Co.
Billey Jackson	10/7/1952	Kidney infection	School Cemetery
Clarence Cunningham	1954	Metastasis to Spinal Cord	Off Campus
George Fordom, Jr.	1/1957	Sarcoma of Lung	Off Campus
Robert J. Hewett	4/4/1960	Gunshot wound	Cypress, FL
Edgar Elton	7/10/1961	Acute Dilation of Heart	Lake Co.
Raymond Phillips	9/15/1961	Shot in Alachua Co.	Alachua Co.
James Fredere	6/10/1965	Auto Accident	Bladen Co.
Alphonso Glover	8/13/1966	Drowned	Off Campus
Martin Williams	4/28/1973	Drowned	Hillsborough Co.

---

[1] J.L. Baldwin, "The Weather of 1944 in the United States," *Monthly Weather Review*, Weather Bureau, Washington, D.C., January 1945, pp. 4-9.

[2] William Foxworth v. Louie L. Wainwright, 516 F. 2d 1072, No. 74-3235, United States Court of Appeals, Fifth Circuit, August 1, 1975. (Hereafter Foxworth v. Wainwright).

[3] *Ibid.*

[4] *Ibid.*

[5] *Dothan Eagle*, November 30, 1944, P. 11.

[6] Foxworth v. Wainwright.

[7] *Ibid.*

[8] "Murder Charged Two in Death of F.I.S. Boy," *Jackson County Floridan*, May 13, 1949, pp. 1 & 10.

[9] *Ibid.*

[10] *Ibid.*

[11] *Ibid.*

[12] Circuit Court Minutes, Jackson County Archives.

[13] "Pupil's Trial opens in Classmate's Death," *Dothan Eagle,* June 2, 1949, P. 1.

[14] Frank Murphy v. Louie Wainwright, 372 F. 2d 942, 5th Circuit U.S. Court of Appeals, February 2, 1967.

[15] *Ibid.*

[16] *Ibid.*

[17] *Ibid.*

[18] Florida Industrial School for Boys Ledgers, Florida State Archives; FDLE Report.

[19] FDLE Report, P. 16.

[20] USF Interim Report, P. 75.

[21] Laura Hair, M.D., and Leszek Chrostowski, M.D., to Erin Kimmerle, Ph.D., October 18, 2012, included in USF Interim Report, pp. 108-109.

[22] Florida Industrial School for Boys Ledgers, Florida State Archives.

[23] *Ibid.*

[24] *Jackson County Floridan.*

[25] *Ibid.*; FDLE Report, P. 16; Cemetery Survey, Antioch Cemetery, Alachua County, Florida, U.S. Genweb.

[26] FDLE Report, Page 15; Cemetery Survey, Garden of Memories Cemetery, Kelly, North Caroina, U.S. Genweb.

[27] FDLE Report, Page 15; USF Interim Report, Page 68; Dale Cox, "USF Researchers refuse to examine Dozier documents," Jackson County, Florida blog (http://twoegg.blogspot.com), October 22, 2013 (reprinted in the appendices of this volume).

[28] Testimony of James N. Smith, Coroner's report on the death of Alphonso Glover, prepared by County Judge J.E. Laramore, August 15, 1966.

[29] *Ibid.*

[30] Testimony of Student Eyewitness #1 [name withheld by author], Coroner's report on the death of Alphonso Glover, prepared by County Judge J.E. Laramore, August 15, 1966.

[31] Testimony of Student Eyewitness #2 [name withheld by author], Coroner's report on the death of Alphonso Glover, prepared by County Judge J.E. Laramore, August 15, 1966.

[32] Coroner's report on the death of Alphonso Glover, prepared by County Judge J.E. Laramore, August 15, 1966.

[33] *Ibid.*

[34] USF Interim Report, Page 74.

[35] *Ibid.*

[36] Laura Hair, M.D., and Leszek Chrostowsi, M.D. to Erin Kimmerle, Ph.D., October 18, 2012, included in USF Interim Report, pp. 108-109.

[37] USF Interim Report, Page 74.

[38] "Final Response" on Case Numbers EI-04-0005 & EI-73-8455, Florida Department of Law Enforcement, Office of Executive Investigations, December 18, 2012.

[39] Ben Montgomery, "Mother agonizes over beating at Florida School for Boys that she says killed her son," *St. Petersburg Times*, September 13, 2009.

[40] Obituary, *The Yellow Jacket*, December 27, 1947; Personal Communication from Robert Daffin, November 11, 2014.

YELLOW JACKETS BASKETBALL TEAM, 1952.

UNDEFEATED TIGERS OF 1951. THE SCHOOL'S ATHLETIC TEAMS PLAYED HIGH
SCHOOL TEAMS FROM THROUGHOUT FLORIDA.

SOUTH CAMPUS BOY SCOUTS IN EARLY 1950S.

NORTH CAMPUS BOY SCOUTS IN EARLY 1950S.

ARTHUR G. DOZIER COUNSELS TWO STUDENTS.

SCHOOL MARCHING BAND PERFORMS DURING WORLD WAR II.

SUPT. ARTHUR G. DOZIER BY A CHRISTMAS DECORATION IN THE 1950S.

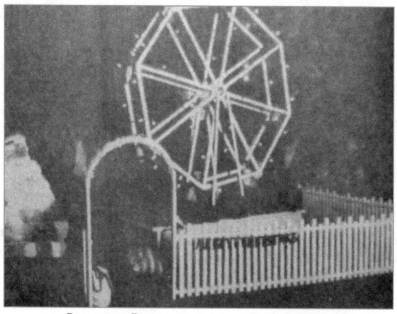

CHRISTMAS DECORATION AT THE BOYS SCHOOL.

DECORATIONS LINE THE ENTRANCE ROAD IN THE 1950S.

CHILDREN OF EMPLOYEES ENJOY A CHRISTMAS PARTY.

Nine

Exhumation

SIXTY YEARS AFTER THE LAST GRAVE WAS PLACED THERE, the University of South Florida initiated a project to survey the Dozier School Cemetery using ground penetrating radar. The objective of the university's researchers was to determine the extent of the cemetery and the number of graves contained within its limits. They also received state permission to look for hidden or "clandestine" graves elsewhere on campus.

News of the university's interest had been received in Jackson County in 2011 when a confidential source informed the author that a researcher at USF had read a book titled *The Bone Yard* by writer Jefferson Bass. The cover image included a representation of the metal crosses at the Dozier School Cemetery and the novel's lead character – Dr. Bill Brockton – uncovers a history of atrocities at a place dubbed the "North Florida Boys Reformatory."[1]

The book was a work of fiction and one in a series of novels by the author. The "North Florida Boys Reformatory" was clearly based on Dozier School for Boys. The school had attracted widespread attention in 2008 when a group of former students came forward to allege that they had been severely beaten and in some cases sexually abused at Dozier. Some of them also alleged that students had been murdered by employees and were buried at "Boot Hill." Governor Charlie Crist directed the Florida Department of Law Enforcement (FDLE) to investigate these claims on December 9, 2008.[2]

Widespread reports of abuse, murders and hidden graves at Dozier School had appeared in the media by this time. Many of the former students were parties to a class action lawsuit filed against the state and former school employee Troy

Tidwell. The case was dismissed with prejudice – meaning it could not be re-filed – by a South Florida judge because the statute of limitations for such action had expired. Most of the allegations that came to light for the first time in 2008 involved events that had allegedly taken place on campus in the 1950s and 1960s. The judge did not rule on the merits of the claims in dismissing the lawsuit.

Great attention was focused on the outcome of the FDLE investigation as it went forward in 2009 and early 2010. Multiple investigators from the agency came to Marianna and spent days on end sifting through the records of the school, interviewing both former students and former employees, and carrying out an on-the-ground examination of the cemetery.[3]

The investigators ultimately determined that 85 people had died at the school in 1911-1973. Of this number, 31 were known to be buried in the small cemetery, 31 were confirmed to have been returned home or were determined to have been buried elsewhere and 23 additional names were located for which burial locations were unknown. FDLE was aware of the 11 students and one employee that died during the Spanish influenza pandemic of 1918, but did not include them in its tally because the investigators could not identify the victims name and was unsure if at least some of them were already included in the agency's total. If the 12 flu victims were added to the agency's list of 85, then the final number of known deaths at the school as determined by FDLE was 97. As FDLE expected, however, some of the flu victims were among the deceased for whom names could be determined.[4]

The agency has often been misquoted in the media as determining that there were only 31 graves at the Dozier School Cemetery. This is incorrect. What FDLE actually reported was that it had confirmed the names of 31 people positively known to have been buried in the cemetery. The agency never said those 31 were the only people buried there:

Given these facts [i.e. information on the original placement of the memorial crosses], the number of crosses placed in the cemetery was not found to be of significance with regard to ascertaining an accurate count of the number of persons buried at this location.[5]

FDLE identified 23 additional people that had died either at Dozier School or in association with the school for whom it could not determine places of burial, exclusive of flu victims not identified by name on its list. Agents of the agency informed the author as early as 2008 that it was very possible that some or all of these individuals were buried in the cemetery. When these 23 names are added to the agency's list of those positively known to have been buried in the cemetery, the tally rises to 53.[6]

The author joined with two other private researchers during the spring and summer of 2009 in an effort to determine whether any of the 23 individuals identified by FDLE for whom no burial locations were known could actually be interred at "Boot Hill." Early in that process we knew for certain that 31 individuals, Sue the peacock and two dogs were buried in the cemetery. As our documentary research went forward, additional names began to surface and were added to the list. By the late summer of 2012 we were able to confirm 31 positive and 22 probable burials in the cemetery. These numbers, indicating a probable total of 53 graves, were publicly announced in September 2012.[7]

The University of South Florida released the interim report on its search at the school on December 10, 2012. Using ground penetrating radar and trenching, the researchers were able to locate 35 "probable grave shafts" and 15 "possible grave shafts." The university's total number of 50 was slightly smaller than our group's determination of 53 probable graves in the cemetery.[8]

USF advocated for exhumation of the graves, an idea that FDLE had opposed. State investigators, in fact, had predicted that any effort to identify the bodies by digging up the graves would likely prove very difficult:

...[T]he physical condition of the remains would make specific identification unlikely. There is no known evidence that any of the deceased were embalmed or buried in sealed or structurally sound caskets. The possibility of confirming identification based on DNA may be difficult due to the burial conditions alongside other contributing factors including advanced decomposition, environmental elements, passage of time and a deficiency of suitable familial candidates for comparison.[9]

FDLE investigators also cautioned that exhuming graves in the State of Florida required a court order issued by a judge based on an affidavit specifying a compelling legal reason for digging up the graves, a "reasonable likelihood" that examination of the remains would reveal pertinent information, and a forensic expert's opinion that evidence might be obtained. The agency's representatives also pointed out that previous exhumation orders in Florida had "acknowledged and addressed conflicts raised by religious beliefs and the feelings of family members and friends as it relates to the exhumation process."[10]

The FDLE investigators were clear in their opinion that little would be learned by digging up the graves:

It does not appear that the results of the investigation support the issuance of any exhumation orders. The investigation did not reveal evidence to suggest that any of the deceased died as a result of criminal conduct which had not been previously investigated. Therefore it is highly unlikely that an autopsy would reveal any information relevant to the investigation.[11]

That the scientists at the University of South Florida disagreed with the seasoned criminal investigators at the Florida Department of Law Enforcement was evident. The university immediately began working with the offices of Florida's Attorney General Pam Bondi and the Medical Examiner for the 14th Judicial Circuit, Dr. Michael Hunter, to seek a court order allowing the exhumation of the entire Dozier School Cemetery. A growing media frenzy served as the backdrop to this effort.

Ignoring the caution provided by FDLE that religious beliefs and the feelings of family and friends should be taken into consideration, as well as the agency's warning that "a deficiency of suitable familial candidates for comparison" would likely make identification using DNA difficult, the university-led effort moved forward. Statewide Prosecutor Nick Cox of the Attorney General's office prepared and filed a petition with the Circuit Court of the 14th Judicial Circuit seeking an order that would grant Dr. Hunter permission to dig up the cemetery. He, in turn, would rely on USF to conduct the project. The petition was filed without first holding any public meeting on the matter or discussing the project with either the City or County Commission.

The result was an explosion of controversy in Marianna and Jackson County. Many in the community were irate that none of the parties involved in the plan to dig up the cemetery had communicated with the public on the matter. Others expressed fear that Jackson County would be forced to pay the cost of the project. A third group was alarmed over the plan to dig up so many Christian burials without the permission of more than 80% of the families of those buried there.

The Jackson County Board of County Commissioners voted unanimously to file a motion to intervene in the matter. The goal of the commissioners – media hyperbole aside – was not to stop the project or, as the *Tampa Bay Times* suggested, to keep the "truth" buried. The commissioners actually sought only two things in their court filing: 1) clarification on responsibility of paying the cost of the project, and 2) the protection of the due process rights of the next of kin of those buried in the Dozier School Cemetery. Despite widespread media claims that USF had secured the permission of the families of those buried in the cemetery, the university at this time had located only seven of the more than fifty next of kin. The county's motion to intervene was granted.[12]

Learning of the vote by the county commission, Statewide Prosecutor (Nick) Cox requested a private meeting with the author and County Attorney Frank Baker to discuss the matter. The conference took place at Baker's office on Lafayette Street in Marianna. Present were the author, the statewide prosecutor and the medical examiner, Dr. Hunter. County Attorney Baker participated in the meeting at times, but was not present for the entire discussion. The atmosphere was cordial and professional.

The discussion began with (Nick) Cox offering an apology on behalf of Attorney General Pam Bondi for failing to discuss the plan to dig up the cemetery with the county commission and citizens of Jackson County prior to the filing of the petition. He indicated that the Attorney General, Ms. Bondi, was willing to come to Marianna to offer a similar message in person. He also expressed his personal support for the idea of convening a forum at Chipola College in Marianna that would be carried live on the college's television station as a way of allowing local residents to learn more about and better understand the proposed project.[13]

A promise was made that no county funds would be required to fund the project and the prosecutor then asked what could be done to resolve the county commission's remaining concerns. Attorney Baker and I explained that it was the wish of the board and many citizens in the community that as many of the next of kin as possible of those buried in the cemetery be located before the project began. (Nick) Cox suggested that a qualified genealogist could be employed for that purpose.

Because of media statements attributed to members of the USF research team, Baker and I requested that the genealogist suggested by the prosecutor be independent of the university. We also requested that an independent professional be appointed to monitor the USF team's work, suggesting State Archaeologist Mary Glowacki or a competent professional from the University of Florida, Florida State University or University of West Florida.

The discussion then turned to the exhumations themselves. Assurance was sought from the statewide prosecutor that no digging up of graves would take place without an appropriate order from the circuit court. Dr. Hunter, the Medical Examiner, intervened at this point and assured us that his office would not participate in the exhumations without a court order. Prosecutor Cox asked for an explanation and Dr. Hunter outlined the position of the statewide organization of Medical Examiners that cemetery burials should not be disturbed without an order from a court of proper jurisdiction. The prosecutor responded with a simple, "Ok."

The meeting concluded with a tentative agreement that a genealogist would be hired to locate next of kin, that the various parties would participate in a televised forum to better inform the community and that no exhumations would take place without a court order. The statewide prosecutor also agreed to submit the idea of an independent monitor to Attorney General Bondi for consideration.[14]

Feeling that their community and reputations were under attack, an overflow audience of Jackson County citizens attended the next meeting of the Board of County Commissioners. The discussion began when representatives of the NAACP appeared before the commissioners to urge that the graves be exhumed. Based on USF's interim report, a belief had developed in some circles by this time that all of the individuals buried in the "Boot Hill" cemetery were African American and that a second "white cemetery" was hidden somewhere else on campus. One of the NAACP representatives went so far as to compare the "White House" at Dozier School to the infamous Nazi death camp at Dachau.

Statewide Prosecutor Nick Cox also appeared before the board, expressing regret that he had not done so before filing the petition for an order to exhume the graves. He indicated that Attorney General Bondi wanted the community to be informed and understand the project. He also told the commissioners that a productive meeting had taken place the previous week with me and County Attorney Frank Baker and assured them that communication would improve in the future. It was his last appearance before the board and as of the publication date of this volume, no other representatives of the Attorney General's office have appeared before the county commission.

The media coverage continued to grow more and more sensational. The *Tampa Bay Times* published a story about the commission's intervention under the headline, "While some seek to uncover the truth, others try to bury it." Some local citizens interviewed for the article later said that they had been misquoted or that their comments were taken out of context. The article did include a statement from me indicating that I believed there were at least 53 graves in the Dozier School Cemetery.

CNN and other news agencies joined the frenzy by reporting "allegations" that the cemetery was a "dumping ground" used by the Ku Klux Klan. These claims were raised with Statewide Prosecutor (Nick) Cox who indicated that the Attorney General's office did not believe such allegations.[15]

(Nick) Cox did facilitate a meeting at the Jackson County Courthouse between the author and Glen Varnadoe, nephew of Thomas Varnadoe who died and was buried at the school in 1934. I indicated to Mr. Varnadoe that I had no objection to him retrieving the remains of his family member, but that I did object to digging up all of the other dead in the process without first obtaining the permission of their next of kin too. He did indicate to me during the meeting that he felt he had been misquoted slightly about the cemetery matter.[16]

By way of explanation, Mr. Varnadoe indicated that he had visited Dozier School for Boys during the 1980s to learn more about the burial site of his uncle. A school employee took him up to "Boot Hill" and showed him the crosses there. The two then traveled back down the hill and up another road to a second spot. Although he was quoted by both the media and USF as indicated that he had been shown two different burial sites, Mr. Varnadoe told me that he could not be sure that he had not simply seen two sides of the same cemetery.[17]

Circuit Judge William Wright denied the petition seeking an exhumation order on May 24, 2013. In doing so he pointed out that Florida did not have an overall law governing the exhumation of human remains, but noted that the State Archaeologist, the State Attorney and the Medical Examiner all had different levels of authority under the law. He also stated that the information included in USF's interim report did not rise to the standard required for a civil case:

...In this case, the Interim Report does not meet the threshold for an order allowing exhumation or autopsy in a civil case because it does not indicate what physical evidence is reasonably expected to be found or how it may prove the cause of death or the identity of the remains, and the family members have not been afforded due process because many of those persons have not been identified or contacted.[18]

In his summary, Judge Wright concluded:

The Petition to Exhume Human Bodies/Remains is denied because if an order is required, there has been no threshold showing of the anticipated evidence necessary in a civil case. The Medical Examiner has statutory authority to conduct investigations, and the State Attorney has the authority to pursue autopsies when necessary. There are current Florida laws in place on handling unmarked graves and moving buried human remains.[19]

In conclusion, the judge warned petitioners to step lightly if they decided to go forward with the project:

...Regardless of the authority to continue this investigation, Florida officials should proceed with caution and pay heed to Currier v. Woodlawn Cemetery, *300 N.Y. 162, 90 N.E.2d 18 (1949)*

> "The quiet of the grave, the repose of the dead, are not lightly to
> be disturbed. Good and substantial reasons must be shown before
> disinterment is to be sanctioned."[20]

In response to the order denying the petition, Florida Attorney General Pam Bondi convened discussions with "interested parties." Neither the Jackson County Commission nor its representatives were invited to participate. The result of these discussions was a decision that USF would apply for an archaeological permit granting its team authority to begin digging up the graves. The university subsequently filed a request with the state for a 1A-32 permit allowing it to proceed.

Dr. Mary Glowacki, Chief of the Bureau of Archaeological Research and State Archaeologist for Florida, responded with a request for additional information on June 13, 2013. In specific, Dr. Glowacki pointed out that the university had not yet submitted the final report for its previous survey of the cemetery and asked numerous detailed questions about the proposed project.[21]

The USF researchers responded on July 8, 2013. While many of the questions and answers were technical in nature, several of the team's responses were noteworthy. For example, when asked by Dr. Glowacki what efforts had been made to determine the extent to which identification of poorly preserved remains might be possible, the researchers replied:

...[W]e anticipate preservation of human remains to be moderate-to-good. Moreover, in cases where human remains were separated from the soil matrix, such as in a wooden casket or other container, and so not subject to bioturbation (such as root action), we can expect good-to-excellent preservation.[22]

In response to a question about procedures for chain of custody of physical evidence, the team responded:

While we maintain specific standard operating procedures for handling evidence to maintain and protect chain of custody for physical evidence in all our work...this is a bioarchaeological investigation – not a criminal case, nor is Boot Hill Cemetery considered a crime scene; therefore, there is no immediate concern for chain of custody.[23]

The researchers also sought clarification from the State Archaeologist on a number of her questions. The response came seven days later from Florida's Secretary of State Ken Detzner.

In a letter to USF researchers Erin Kimmerle and Christian Wells, Secretary Detzner pointed out that they were seeking a third archaeological permit while they still had two incomplete projects underway on the Dozier School. Reminding them that the permits had been issued for the purpose of locating the gravesites so the school cemetery could be preserved "as a valuable historical resource for Florida and surviving family members," he questioned the direction of their work:

Your inquiry diverged from its original objectives when you sought a third permit with the purpose of actually exhuming the bodies from their grave sites. The Department of State does not have the statutory authority to fulfill your request. The [Bureau of Archaeological Research's] existing statutory authority to grant archaeological research permits is restricted to the recovery of objects of historical or archaeological value, not human remains, absent a danger to the grave site that actually threatens the loss or damage of those remains.[24]

Detzner informed Kimmerle and Wells that the Department of State lacked the statutory authority to grant a permit allowing them to exhume the graves and accordingly could take no action on their request:

...Under Florida law, human bodies are not objects to be dug up for research purposes. To the contrary, the law presumes that buried human remains will rest undisturbed, and allows their intentional disinterment only in narrowly defined circumstances for which specific procedures are provided in law.[25]

The decision by Secretary Detzner was coupled with a decision by the Medical Examiner that he would not participate in the planned exhumation of the graves. Dr. Hunter had previously clarified that he would not go forward with involvement in the dig unless it was authorized with a court order. While his office did later fulfil its statutory responsibility by helping to return three sets of remains to their families, he ended his involvement in the actual exhumations. Glenn Hess, the State Attorney for the 14th Judicial Circuit, had already decided based on the FDLE investigation that there was not sufficient evidence for his office to become further involved.[26]

Pushed by Attorney General Pam Bondi, the issue now landed in the laps of the elected members of the Florida Cabinet. A political and media issue as much as an anthropological one, the exhumation project was approved by Bondi and the other Cabinet officers. USF was given one year to complete its work on the campus.

The dig at "Boot Hill" began on Labor Day Weekend in 2013. With CNN providing live coverage, *Tampa Bay Times* writer Ben Montgomery given special access, and even a 9-year-old child helping with the work, the team from the University of South Florida started its project – and quickly discovered that the water table in the hill was much higher than expected. Trenches filled with water and the researchers worked in mud as they tried to exhume the first of the graves.

The local media was kept back from the site but word soon spread in Marianna that the work was going much slower than expected. With that bit of detail also came news that the researchers were not finding what they had expected. Instead of a mass grave or the bodies of murdered children thrown into holes, the USF team found evidence that the graves had been prepared according to religious and mortuary practices of the time. Hardware from coffins and even pins from burial shrouds were discovered. Contrary to the expectations of the team that remains buried in coffins would be in "good-to-excellent condition," the remains were badly deteriorated. The coffins themselves had all but completely disappeared during the more than 60 years they had spent in the soil of "Boot Hill," leaving behind little more than handles, nails and other bits of hardware.

The researchers came and went through the fall and into the winter of 2013. Following the initial weekend of work, however, their attitude about the media changed. USF decided to bar all press from the site except during organized media events. No explanation was given for this change but it was confirmed by the office of the university's General Counsel.[27]

In September 2013 the author located documentation that two deaths had taken place at the Florida Reform School in 1901-1906. Since neither the FDLE investigation nor the USF research had located this information, it was provided to the university. The document did not include information on the burial location of the two students and raised the possibility that they might have been buried in the cemetery, raising the total potential number of graves there to 55.[28]

The discovery of the obituary for Superintendent Morgan a short time later temporarily raised the possibility that there might be 56 graves at "Boot Hill." His grave was located at Riverside Cemetery in Marianna, however, discounting that possibility.

USF stoked controversy in Marianna's historical community during October 2013, even as the work of exhuming the graves went forward. The situation developed when researcher Antoinette Jackson contacted Pat Crisp of the Chipola Historical Trust to request a meeting and the chance to review any Dozier-related documents that might be in the possession of the Trust. It was the first time that USF reached out to the local historical group in more the one year of research and activity on the Dozier campus.[29]

The organization did not have any documents pertaining to Dozier School in its collections so in an effort to be helpful Mrs. Crisp reached out to the author to ask if Dr. Jackson and others might look at the material that the research group with which I was associated had assembled. I agreed and offered as a courtesy to box pertinent material and bring it to Marianna to make it more easily accessible to the researches.[30]

That evening I placed files containing thousands of pages of documents into four large boxes. Included were obituaries, grand jury reports, coroner's jury testimony and findings, law enforcement reports, hospital records, historical photographs, letters, newspaper articles, copies of school documents and other material that I had not seen referenced in USF's interim report. I was willing to allow the researchers full access to the material and the opportunity to copy any items that they wished.

Per my agreement with Mrs. Crisp I took the material to the archives area in the basement of the Jackson County Courthouse and waited there for her and the researchers to arrive. They were meeting at a Marianna restaurant for lunch. After a wait of approximately two hours, Mrs. Crisp arrived alone and indicated that Dr. Jackson and the USF researchers had refused to look at the documentation. This stunned not only me but the county employees present at the time as well.

Later that day I issued the following statement:

Not only is this sad, it is silly. It is hard for me to imagine that any serious researcher would turn down the chance to view a collection containing thousands of pages of documentation on a topic of such interest to them. But, sadly, that is the case with USF.

The school apparently would rather remain in the dark than so much as talk politely with someone who disagrees with them and their tactics. Perhaps the researchers would do well to learn that people can be polite, even though they disagree with you.[31]

The research team continued its work in the cemetery, still operating under the mistaken belief that all of the graves there contained the remains of African Americans. On the same day a member of the team told a local citizen with regard to the "Boot Hill" site, "This is the black cemetery." A second member of the team told a different individual that day that the project was about "social justice," an area in which she hoped to continue to work in the future.[32]

The fallacy of that belief was exposed when the dig team suddenly exposed bits and pieces of charred human bone, clearly the remains of the unfortunate students and employees that died in the dormitory fire on November 18, 1914. All of those individuals were white. The university at first did not disclose this information publicly but finally did so in a report of its search for the alleged "second cemetery" on the South or "white" campus of the school:[33]

...That not all of the victims of the fire were interred in the Boot Hill Burial Ground suggests the possibility that some of the individuals may have been buried along with fire debris at the South Campus dormitory site. Prospection with a bucket auger in this area...has revealed the location of the dormitory, but large scale clearing (e.g., with the use of heavy equipment) is necessary to locate any possible clandestine gave [sic.] sites.[34]

The researchers did not state how many victims of the fire they had located in graves at "Boot Hill," but the likely reason that they did not find all of them was that the university had over-estimated the number who died in the 1914 tragedy. As was noted in Chapter Two herein, USF included names in its Interim Report of two people that did not exist. This error was based on a newspaper misprint and a mistake in a document at the Jackson County Courthouse. Both sources quickly corrected their mistakes, but the research team evidently did not see the corrections. Correction of these errors lowers the estimated death toll from the fire from 12 as claimed by USF in its interim report to 10, the number reported in virtually every newspaper of the time. In addition, it was discovered soon after the fire that one student thought to have died in the blaze had actually used the chaos as an opportunity to escape. He was arrested in Georgia, lowering the number of victims to nine. A second student, Waldo Drew, was thought to have died in the fire, but his remains could not be found. These changes indicated that there should have been no more than 8 sets of remains from the fire buried at "Boot Hill," not the 12 anticipated by USF.[35]

The last of the bodies from the cemetery were exhumed during the winter of 2013. The final number located was 55, the same number anticipated in advance by the author's research team. As of the publication of this book, the University of South Florida has succeeded in identifying only 3 of the 55 bodies that it exhumed. It has confirmed that 5 other bodies could not be identified using DNA comparisons. Other sources indicate that an additional body, thought to be that of Samuel Morgan, could not be positively identified because the relatives from whom researchers took DNA samples were not close enough in relationship for a match. Two of the three bodies identified as of this writing were white. One was African American.[36]

Reports that bodies were found under roads or well away from the known cemetery are false. The remains exhumed by USF were inside the historic cemetery as defined by a quadrangular gated fence that once surrounded the site. All of the graves were within a small area measuring approximately 75 feet by 100 feet. They were in rows and all of the bodies had been buried facing east according to standard religious practices of the 20th Century.[37]

---

[1] Personally communicated to the author by a confidential source, August 2011; Jefferson Bass, *The Bone Yard: A Body Farm Novel*, HarperCollins Publishers, 2011.

[2] "Investigative Summary," Arthur G. Dozier School for Boys Abuse Investigation, Case No. EI-04-0005, Florida Department of Law Enforcement, January 29, 2010, Page 1; Kate MCardell, "Historian: Graves mark flu epidemic victims," *Jackson County Floridan*, December 12, 2008.

[3] For the results of FDLE's investigation of the abuse allegations, please see "Investigative Summary," Arthur G. Dozier School for Boys Abuse Investigation, Case No. EI-04-0005, Florida Department of Law Enforcement, January 29, 2010.

[4] 'Final response,' Arthur G. Dozier School for Boys Investigation, Case No. EI-04-0005 & EI-73-8455, Florida Department of Law Enforcement, December 18, 2012.

[5] *Ibid.*

[6] *Ibid.*; Personal communication to author, March 5, 2009.

[7] "Southern Heritage" program, CCTV, September 12, 2012.

[8] USF Interim Report, Page 34.

[9] "Investigative Summary," Cemetery investigation at Arthur G. Dozier School for Boys, Case No. E-73-8455, Florida Department of Law Enforcement, May 14, 2009, Page 17.

[10] *Ibid.*

[11] *Ibid.*

[12] Personal notes of the author.

[13] *Ibid.*

[14] *Ibid.*

[15] Personal notes of the author.

[16] *Ibid.*

[17] *Ibid.*

[18] Order Denying Petition, In Re: Exhumation of Unidentified Human Remains Buried at the Dozier School for Boys, Case No.: 13-239 CA, signed by Hon. William Wright, Circuit Judge, May 24, 2013.

[19] *Ibid.*

[20] *Ibid.*

[21] Mary Glowacki, Ph.D. to Erin Kimmerle Ph.D., Christian Wells, Ph.D. *et al*, June 14, 2013.

[22] Erin Kimmerle, Ph.D. and E. Christian Wells, Ph.D. to Mary Glowacki, Ph.D., July 8, 2013.

[23] *Ibid.*

[24] Secretary of State Ken Detzner to Erin Kimmerle, Ph.D. and Christian Wells, Ph.D., July 15, 2013.

[25] *Ibid.*

[26] Personal Communication from Dr. Michael Hunter, 2013.

[27] Personal Communication from Girard Solis, 2013.

[28] Dale Cox to Gerard Solis, September 2013.

[29] Pat Crisp to Dale Cox, October 21, 2013.

[30] Dale Cox to Pat Crisp, October 21, 2013.

[31] Dale Cox, "USF researchers refuse to examine Dozier documents," Jackson County, Florida blog, http://twoegg.blogspot.com, October 22, 2013.

[32] Personal communication from confidential informants, October 22, 2013.

[33] E. Christian Wells, Erin H. Kimmerle & Antoinette T. Jackson, "Archaeological Prospection of Possible Clandestine Graves on the South Campus of the Arthur G. Dozier School for Boys, Marianna, Florida," Archaeological Research Permit (Chapter 1A-32) Report, Permit No. 1213.018, Department of Anthropology, University of South Florida, July 8, 2014, Page 4 (hereafter USF South Campus Report).

[34] *Ibid.*

[35] See Chapter Two herein for a history of the 1914 fire.

[36] Press releases of the University of South Florida, 2014; Personal communication from confidential informant, August 11, 2014.

[37] Erin Kimmerle, Ph.D. and E. Christian Wells, Ph.D. to Mary Glowacki, Ph.D., July 8, 2013; USF Interim Report, Page 34.

MEMORIAL CROSSES IN 1990.

MEMORIAL CROSSES AT DOZIER CEMETERY IN 2013.

DOZIER SCHOOL CEMETERY IN 2013. THE ENTIRE BURIAL SITE MEASURED
ROUGHLY 75-FEET BY 100-FEET. THE CROSSES IN THE BACKGROUND WERE
PLACED AS A MEMORIAL.

SPOIL PILE LEFT BY USF AFTER USING HEAVY EQUIPMENT ON TOP OF THE
CEMETERY. WIRE FROM THE ORIGINAL CEMETERY FENCE CAN BE SEEN.

ARTIFACT LEFT BEHIND IN TIRE TRACK OF USF VEHICLE, 2013.

Ten

"Clandestine Graves"

THE SUBTITLE OF THIS VOLUME IS "The Attempted Assassination of an American City." This is not a reference to the University of South Florida or even to the controversy that surrounded its project to exhume the graves at Dozier School. It is a reference to the media and specifically to the scores of state, national and international media outlets that published and/or broadcast unsubstantiated claims that hidden cemeteries and clandestine graves existed in numerous specific locations on the school campus.

The implication was that the employees of Dozier School for Boys had murdered scores of juvenile students and buried their bodies in hidden locations. The reputation of the City of Marianna was seriously damaged by these reports which gave little if any consideration to the possibility that the claims might not be true.

The allegations of hidden burials at Dozier School were given prominent consideration in USF's interim report. The university operated for some time on the theory that there must have been two cemeteries on campus because of the societal rules of the Jim Crow era. "It would have been common, prior to integration," the researchers wrote, "for whites and coloreds to be buried in separate or segregated cemeteries."[1]

The theory advanced by many and accepted at least in part by the university was that the known Dozier School Cemetery on "Boot Hill" was the site where students from the "colored" or African American campus were buried prior to desegregation. Local residents and former employees of the school denied this, pointing out that no one in the community had ever heard of a second cemetery. Some questioned the obviously faulty logic of the idea, questioning why – during the Jim Crow era – Southern white employees of the school would have marked and preserved the African American cemetery while hiding and failing to care for the "white" cemetery. If this had really happened at Dozier School it would have been a reversal of virtually all that we know of the segregation era.

Logic aside, belief in a second cemetery became widespread throughout the nation thanks to interviews given by USF researchers, former students and even a United States Senator. An organization of former students, for example, issued a statement as early as December 8, 2008, describing the known cemetery as a "mass grave site" and suggesting that researchers would find "more mass graves surrounding the facility."[2]

One former student in particular repeatedly maintained that there was a second cemetery on the South Campus. In various anonymous online posts, he indicated that he had pointed out and flagged the site of the "white cemetery" in an area behind the chimneys of the school's industrial plant for USF researchers.[3]

Others pointed out other locations. Cemeteries were supposed to hidden behind the "White House," near the administration building, behind staff cottages, beneath a swimming pool, 2,000 feet from "Boot Hill," and on a parcel roughly one-mile north of the known cemetery. So many people claimed there were hidden cemeteries in so many places it is remarkable that anyone survived their time at the school. Researchers from USF even started considering other locations where potential clandestine cemeteries might be located, including one in the author's neighborhood more than 20 miles from campus.[4]

In fairness to the research team, some of the belief in a second cemetery was fostered by the statements of two relatives of students known to have been buried on campus.

Glen Varnadoe is the nephew of Thomas Varnadoe, who died at the school in 1934. He told researchers that he had been shown two different areas on campus that were reported to be gravesites. In a personal conversation with the author, however, he volunteered that he could not say for sure that he had not seen two different sides or parts of the known "Boot Hill" cemetery. This honest observation by Mr. Varnadoe was clearly correct as his uncle's remains are among those from "Boot Hill" that have been identified through DNA comparison by the University of North Texas.[5]

Ovell Krell is the sister of George Owen Smith who died during the winter of 1940-1941. According to her various statements and in particular the account she gave to USF researchers, Ms. Krell was absolutely convinced that her brother was

126

buried in a cemetery near the administration building on the South campus. She told researchers that the superintendent had taken her and other family members to her brother's graves shortly after his remains were found in 1941. It was in a row of two graves, marked only by mounds of dirt, in an open area near the woods and not far from the administration building. In fairness to Ms. Krell, she was a young girl at the time and had not returned to campus since the visit in 1941. The campus has changed dramatically in the more than 70 years that have passed since she was shown George Smith's grave. New buildings were built, roads were realigned trees were planted, fences were constructed and other dramatic changes made. When researchers at the University of North Texas identified a body from "Boot Hill" as her brother through the use of DNA, it was obvious that Ms. Krell had been mistaken about the location of his burial site. This was clearly not an intentional mistake, though, and was simply due to the passage of time.[6]

There is a lesson to be learned from these two situations. The passage of time plays tricks on the human mind – all human minds. Some call it the fog of history. Eyewitness accounts are notoriously unreliable even in the immediate aftermath of a traumatic event such as a death, let alone when recorded many years later. Shortly before the publication of this volume in 2014, for example, the nation was stunned by the riots that erupted in the city of Ferguson, Missouri. An African American teen had been shot by a Ferguson police officer, but a county grand jury declined to return an indictment. A review of the testimony presented to the grand jury showed that dozens of witnesses had been called, but their stories were almost all different. Some even admitted that they were repeating what they had heard or seen on television. Most, however, honestly believed that events had taken place as they remembered, even though their story was different from other people that saw the same event. If eyewitness testimony is unreliable so close to a traumatic event, it is easy to understand how it can be totally incorrect 60 or 70 years after the fact.

The media made much of claims of hidden graves and secret cemeteries. The Sunshine State News, for example, published a story on July 11, 2013, proclaiming "USF Team May Have Found Dozier School's 'White Cemetery' Site." The report cited USF researcher Dr. E. Christian Wells as the source for the information that the team was going to excavate a site that "they say" could be the "white cemetery." The report by Eric Giunta went on to note that three former students had claimed there once were grave markers on a parcel nearly one mile northeast of the cemetery at "Boot Hill." A forth student told the reporter that he had seen grave markers in another location about 2,000 feet away.[7]

If the quotes in the story are correct, Dr. Wells told the reporter that researchers had talked to 30-40 individuals, each of whom had pointed out a different location where he or she believed hidden graves were located. The researcher told the reporter that the individuals with whom USF was collaborating had said there was a second cemetery. He was quoted directly as saying that the team expected to find two formal cemeteries on campus.[8]

The writer, Eric Giunta, even called into question the claims that whites and blacks had been buried together at "Boot Hill." It would have been, he wrote, contrary to what was done elsewhere in the United States at the time. The reporter evidently did not visit Marianna's Riverside Cemetery or he would have noticed that hundreds of whites and hundreds of African Americans had been buried in the same cemetery from the early 1800s all the way to the present.[9]

U.S. Senator Bill Nelson, always a proponent of exhuming the graves at Dozier School, joined the fray. In comments published by the *Tampa Bay Times* on April 15, 2014, the Senator said that because seven sets of remains from "Boot Hill" had been identified as African American, there was a possibility that all 55 bodies exhumed from the site were black and that a second "white" cemetery existed somewhere on campus. In a video posted on its website in connection with the story, the newspaper even claimed that the known cemetery was "hidden." This was a remarkable allegation since the burial site at "Boot Hill" had been shown on state and federal maps since the 1940s and memorial crosses had been maintained there since the 1960s.[10]

The list of media outlets that published speculation that a second "white" cemetery must exist is long:

> WFTS-TV, Examiner.com, National Public Radio, *Tampa Bay Times*, *The Tampa Tribune*, WMNF-FM, Oregon Public Broadcasting, WCTV-TV, WTVT-TV, Sunshine State News, *The Daily Mail*, Bay Community News, *The Guardian*, Huffingtonpost.com, KHOU-TV, *The Washington Post*, Fox News, Yahoo News, CBS News, NewsMax, Wikipedia, *USA Today*, Associated Press, *The Arizona Republic*, KSL-TV, *The Seattle Times*, *The Daily Herald*, *The Denver Post*, WFLA-TV, WTSP-TV, WJHG-TV, *The Atlanta Journal-Constitution*, KAKE-TV, *The New Hampshire Register*, *The Salt Lake Tribune*, CNN, CNS News, *The Zanesville Times Recorder*, *The Advocate*, KMGH-TV, *The Clarion-Ledger*, *The Star Press*, *The Rapid City Journal*, *The Oakland Press*, *The Epoch Times*, *The New York*

Daily News, The Ocala Post, Sun Sentinel, WJXT-TV, *The Australian,* etc.

The list goes on but there is one error that all of these media outlets had in common – there was no secret "white cemetery" at Dozier School for Boys. The known cemetery on "Boot Hill" contained the remains of 55 individuals. They were white, black and Hispanic. The speculation – and that is all it was – of clandestine graves and hidden second cemeteries amounted to nothing. The nation, indeed the world, was told by media outlets of all stripes that the graves of children murdered by employees likely dotted the landscape of Dozier School and Marianna.

While it is true that the University of South Florida has not searched every square inch of the more than 1,000-acre school property, the university did check all of the locations pointed out to it by those who claimed to have knowledge of "clandestine" graves. Not one single grave was found outside of the 75 by 100 foot area on "Boot Hill" that community residents and former employees had said all along was the only cemetery on campus that they had ever heard mentioned or seen.

The true story began to slowly emerge when USF quietly filed a report about its search for hidden graves on the old South campus on July 8, 2014. The document confirmed that researchers had tested 33 different locations in search of the alleged grave sites pointed out by former students and some family members of deceased students. "We conclude that there are no human burials located in the specific areas we tested," wrote researchers Erin Kimmerle, Ph.D., E. Christian Wells, Ph.D., and Antoinette T. Jackson, Ph.D. [11]

The researchers went on to point out that they had carried out the search on the South Campus because of "legitimate archival evidence and eyewitness accounts" that indicated the presence of possible burial sites there. Specifically they cited Ms. Krell's seven decade old memories of where her brother, George Owen Smith, had been buried. They also credited a former student, Philip Marchesani, who claimed to have seen boxes of letters from parents and school maps showing two separate burial sites. These documents were supposedly stored in the attic of the Chapel. USF has repeatedly claimed they were recovered by the Florida Department of Law Enforcement, a claim that FDLE denies. In the report on their South Campus search, the researchers added a claim that the "materials were destroyed by the Department of Juvenile Justice" but do not cite authority for such an allegation. [12]

Such "legitimate" evidence aside, USF found no evidence of graves, grave shafts or even a place where graves might have once been placed. None of the locations pointed out by former students produced any evidence of hidden burials:

No burial shafts were detected in any of the anomalies tested. However, the research located a number of cultural features, including possible building foundations, pipe lines, and buried trash middens. We also uncovered soil evidence indicating prior trenching and/or land clearance – especially in the area identified by Ms. Krell as well as other witnesses. From these results, we conclude that there are most likely no human interments in the specific areas tested.[13]

The researchers did leave open the possibility that there might be hidden graves in the area where the dormitory burned in 1914. They appeared to base this supposition on their failure to find enough sets of charred remains at "Boot Hill" to match the clearly inflated number of deaths that they believed had resulted from the fire.[14]

So far as can be determined, only three media outlets – all of them local to Northwest Florida – covered the release of this report. The statewide, national and international media never returned to Marianna to set the record straight.

More than two years have passed since the University of South Florida began its work on the campus of Dozier School for Boys. Not one single grave has been found outside of the 75-foot by 100-foot cemetery on "Boot Hill." The researchers are rarely seen in Marianna and the media has disappeared with them. The university still refuses to release emails passed between one member of the media and its lead researcher. Efforts to obtain them using Florida's Sunshine Law and Public Records Statutes have been rebuffed for now.

Scientists at the University of North Texas have been able to use DNA to identify three of the bodies exhumed by USF. Hopefully they will be able to identify a few more. Most of the remains, however, will eventually be given numbers instead of names and placed back in the ground. Perhaps more could be identified had the researchers followed the advice of Judge William Wright and located the families before beginning the project. At last report, more than 80% of the next of kin had still not been found. USF has announced no findings that any of the graves it exhumed contained the remains of children murdered by staff members.

Marianna will survive the attempted assassination it received at the hands of the media. It is well on its way to a prosperous future.

[1] USF Interim Report, Page 32.

[2] Statement by The White House Boys, December 8, 2014.

[3] Anonymous comments posted online, Jackson County Florida blog, http://twoegg.blogspot.com, January 30, 2014.

[4] Various locations reported in media reports; USF researchers spent time at the Jackson County Clerk of Courts' office looking for information on former county school sites, including one less than one mile from my home. They explained that they were looking for the "second cemetery."

[5] See Chapter Six for details on Thomas Varnadoe's death and burial.

[6] See Chapter Seven for details on George Owen Smith's death and burial.

[7] Eric Giunta, "USF Team May Have Found Dozier School's 'White Cemetery' Site," Sunshine State News, www.sunshinestatenews.com, July 11, 2013.

[8] *Ibid.*

[9] *Ibid.*

[10] Ben Montgomery, "Early lab work suggests existence of undiscovered Dozier cemetery" and associated video, *Tampa Bay Times* website (www.tampabay.com), April 15, 2014.

[11] E. Christian Wells, Erin H. Kimmerle & Antoinette T. Jackson, "Archaeological Prospection of Possible Clandestine Graves on the South Campus of the Arthur G. Dozier School for Boys, Marianna, Florida," Archaeological Research Permit (Chapter 1A-32) Report, Permit No. 1213.018, Department of Anthropology, University of South Florida, July 8, 2014 (hereafter USF South Campus Report).

[12] *Ibid.*; "Final Response," Arthur G. Dozier School for Boys, Florida Department of Law Enforcement, Office of Executive Investigations, December 18, 2012.

[13] USF South Campus Report.

[14] See Chapters Two and Nine for more information.

Appendices

Appendix One

Report from the Marianna Times-Courier
Prompted by reports in statewide newspapers that black and white children were eating together and sleeping under the same roof at the Florida Reform School.
November 26, 1903
Singletary Collection

We first went into the department reserved for white children and found everything neat and clean. Their sleeping quarters were supplied with iron beds, with good cotton mattresses, springs and plenty of covering. In the barns were stowed seven hundred bushels of corn and a large quantity of hay, peas, etc., all raised by the children.

We then drove to the colored quarters and after visiting the grounds we went into the sleeping room. We would never have judged from appearances that thirty-seven colored boys occupied the room every night. We are satisfied that not one of the occupants ever before enjoyed such comforts as we found there.

We next visited the kitchen and witnessed the cooking of supper. It was a sight worth seeing – such quantities of meat, potatoes, bread, etc.

On visiting the dining room we found everything splendidly arranged and very clean. We heard a great deal of talking and laughing, and upon going to the door saw the children returning from work. Each one was compelled to bathe his face, head, ears, hands and feet before he was allowed to eat supper. They looked more like a lot of children just out of school than juvenile convicts.

We were convinced that the charges made by several of our exchanges of the white and colored children eating and sleeping together are erroneous and untrue. The races are separated and occupy different quarters. The only time they mingle together is when they are being taught to work in the field, and their school rooms are four hundred yards apart.

Upon going into the fields we found that most of the stumps had been removed. They have enough fattened hogs to kill to furnish 3,500 pounds of meat.

Judging from the way things are progressing, we think that in two years the institution will be self-sustaining.

The superintendent is a man of great force of character, a hard worker and knows how to handle children. He is a good farmer, an excellent school teacher and a fine business man. Through the errors of some one a grave injustice has been done him and the institution. Instead of censure he deserves praise for the manner in which he has conducted the reformatory.

When one child is so bad that two parents can't make him good and have to send him to the reformatory, it is difficult to understand how one superintendent can correct forty-four of them at one time and make them saints.

Appendix Two

Official report on the fatal 1914 dormitory fire
Submitted by Gov. Park Trammell to the Legislature
April 21, 1915
Singletary Collection

In the early morning of November 18, 1914, a disastrous fire occurred in the white school, in which five of the inmates and two employees lost their lives. This Board desires to report the essential facts as brought out from employes and inmates present at the fire, through an exhaustive investigation held by this board two days after the fire.

The superintendent in charge was asleep in his room at the school. The night watchman, whose duty it was to be on duty at that time, was at his post.

Two inmates who were sent to the barn a few hours before the fire occurred, testified to seeing a man, whom they claim to have recognized, run from the barn. Another inmate, who was aroused by the return of these two, remarked that he could see a man near the bakery, and was told by the first two who the man was.

Later an employe went to the lower floor, passing within ten feet of where the fire originated; returning to his room he went again to bed, but before going to sleep "heard a roaring," and on opening his door discovered the fire under considerable headway, near the foot of the east stairway. He gave the alarm, the night watchman promptly unlocked all dormitories and ordered the boys into fire drill formation, taking charge of those from one dormitory.

Other employes then arrived, taking charge of the other line. Both lines were being directed down the west stairway. Of the ninety-five boys in these two dormitories, all those from the section for smaller boys had reached safety, all from the larger boys' section had passed except three.

By this time the stairway had become obscure by smoke and the attendant wrapped a coat around his head, instructing the three remaining boys to do the same and follow him. He dashed down the stairs safely, but these three boys did not follow and were lost.

One smaller boy, known to have been somewhat deficient mentally, ran back after coming to a place of safety and was lost.

One young hero lost his life in an attempt to rescue the acting superintendent, whom it was thought had not been awakened, but who had gained safety by going over the roof. Two employes, father and son, were lost after gaining safety, each going back into the building seeking the other.

One boy reported as lost is known to have run away. It being necessary to keep the inmates in confinement at night, the fire escapes were locked, the keys being in the office on the main floor in a place known to all about the building. However, had these fire escapes been opened and that method of escape adopted, it is the testimony of those present that the rapidity of progress of the fair would have increased, rather than decreased, the casualty loss.

It would be one bright spot in this hideous occurrence if all the deeds of heroism and self-forgetfulness on the part of the boys and employes during the fire, and of the loyalty of the boys to the superintendent and to the institution, might here be recorded.

The Board of Managers had no desire to escape any censure that may justly be theirs in this connection, but simply desire, in view of many conflicting an erroneous reports given publicity, to place the facts before you.

Respectfully submitted,
W.H. Milton,
Chairman, Board of Managers

Appendix Three

Official report of the physician's committee on the Spanish influenza pandemic of 1918.
November 1918
Carswell Collection & Singletary Collection

To the Board of Commissioners of State Institutions, Tallahassee, Florida.

Gentlemen: At your request we have this day visited and inspected conditions at the Florida Industrial School for Boys at Marianna. After a careful survey of the buildings, hospital facilities, sewerage system and general condition of the institution, we respectfully submit our findings as follows:

This institution has just passed through the throes of the recent influenza epidemic, and very few of the inmates, officers and help of the institution escaped its ravages. Out of 247 boys all but three came down with it practically at one time; the assistant superintendent in charge of the colored side, and his whole family. The matron at No. 2 died with it. In fact, very few escaped the ravages of this insidious disease. At one time it was without water, save what was hauled from nearby sources, because all three engineers and the boys who helped them were down sick.

We find that the hospital is very inadequate, being a small wooden building about 16 by 16 feet, with a bath room and toilet attached.

There are two cottages for the white boys, the general plan and construction of which would be a credit to any institution in the state. The arrangement and architectural features are unusually good and the heating and ventilating facilities are all that could be desired and especially adapted to that type of building. With the exception of minor repairs needed to the toilets and lavatories of Cottage No. 1, very little is needed to put these buildings in the best of condition.

We find the bed linen and sleeping dormitories for the white side kept in fairly good shape considering conditions brought about by the recent epidemic. Night clothing and wearing apparel for white boys is inadequate, but material is on hand to make up these articles. All things considered, conditions on the white side are in very good condition.

At school No. 2 for colored boys we find that they are more crowded than on the white side. This department being the first stricken with influenza necessarily suffered most, as the disease during the first three days at this school brought down all but two or three of the inmates and all of the ten attaches except two, the death of the matron being the first to result from the disease. The night clothing and bed linen was inadequate and in poor condition, probably due to the existing conditions previous to the epidemic, but there was material on hand to remedy this shortage. There were a large number of mattresses that were condemned during the epidemic and there are still others that should be replaced by new ones. On account of the shortage of water and help during the epidemic the general condition of the building for the colored boys became very unsanitary, but is now being greatly improved.

We find that there is on hand an ample supply of almost all the necessary food products, the deficiency being the failure to ration it in proper variety. We do not believe that fresh meats and sugars are made a part of their regular ration. This condition could be easily offset as there are plenty of cows and hogs on the place to supply the fresh meats, and the sugars and sweets at the institution only need to be properly distributed. The fault in these particulars is not in any wise chargeable to your honorable board, but to those in charge of the dietary program, this condition being aggravated by the shortage of cooks and attendants during the epidemic.

We find the institution provided with a good electric light plant, adequate water works, with a stand-pipe of 75,000 gallons capacity. A modern dairy is being erected.

The general location of this institution is good, the land being well drained, high, healthful and wholesome.

In our judgment it is necessary and we recommend, that this institution be supplied with a receiving hospital and infirmary services, this being necessary so that all cases received can be isolated, diagnosed and placed in a clean, sanitary condition on admission before being allowed to associate with the other inmates, and that the sick be properly cared for at all times; the immediate purchasing of new mattresses and destroying of all that are soiled, torn and rendered useless at this time; an up-to-date septic disposal sewerage plant, with competent [word illegible] and engineers in charge of same, special attention being given to more modern toilets and plumbing on the colored side, and that a dietitian skilled in the value and preparation of food be employed.

In conclusion, we are glad to say that, while all cases have not been discharged, conditions generally have greatly improved since the abatement of the epidemic, and, all things considered, we feel that the death rate of this institution during the scourge was remarkably low.

Respectfully submitted,
N.A. Baltzell, M.D.
Attending Physician

W.M. Bevis, M.S.
Superintendent
Florida Hospital for the Insane

R.A. Willis, M.S.
State Prison Physician

Appendix Four

Letter from Crawford Jackson, General Secretary of the Juvenile Protective Association of Atlanta, to the Florida Legislature.
April 2, 1919
Singletary Collection

Gentlemen: - Since my boyhood residence in Florida I have had an increasing interest in the state, and I trust during the last score of years, a more intelligent and worth-while interest...Today, in company with Rev. J.W. Senterfitt, of Marianna, I have made a careful, thorough and unbiased investigation of the Florida Industrial School for Boys three miles from this city.

And instead of addressing your honorable body in person, as I have been told that I ought to do, I prefer – even though an authoritative invitation should be extended me – to reach you and as many of your constituents as possible through the generosity of the press, and submit for consideration the following suggestions:

1. [Recommended raising salaries of employees.]

2. Some of your number, as well as prominent citizens here and there, have requested me to give my views as to the present status of the Florida Industrial School visited and studied today. This school, as you well know, has received from all quarters the severest criticism, and much of it has been just, but I am glad indeed to tell you that I was greatly surprised after going carefully, and unexpectedly to the management, through every department of this institution. Some marked improvements have been made and more are contemplated. The legislative committee of the last session, visiting, investigating and reporting as to its conditions and needs, has brought forth good fruit. But that institution cannot become the best saving constructive factor possible for the class of children who are sent there unless it has an adequate equipment which embraces the buildings, machinery, of an up-to-date school and every man and woman connected with it as an employe an expert in his or her line. If this institution has been wayward, let us see to it that we give the school the same chance to make good that we would offer to the wayward child

and such opportunities, so far as possible, as we would give our own children if they became delinquent.

New buildings are going up at this industrial school and old ones being overhauled. Dr. Frank E. McClane, the new superintendent, is ambitious to do the best possible for the school and the state, and he has already begun to make good.

I deplore the fact that there are boys now of six, or seven years associating, more or less, with those of eighteen, nineteen and twenty; but the cottage system, already beginning to be put into operation, is to be further extended so that the more wayward, as well as the older boys, will be separated from the less wayward and the younger ones. I cannot ask for the space in this paper to go into details as to the needs of this institution, but I beg of you to make just as ample provision for it comparatively as you would for any other institution under state control. And let the law be further amended, as Dr. McClane suggests, so that the boys will be sent by the courts to the school not as a punishment for wrong doing, but as an inducement to make good....

Appendix Five

Letter from Secretary of State Ken Detzner to USF researchers.
July 15, 2013
Author's Collection

FLORIDA DEPARTMENT *of* STATE

RICK SCOTT
Governor

KEN DETZNER
Secretary of State

July 15, 2013

Via email and U.S. Mail

Dr. Erin H. Kimmerle, Associate Professor
Dr. E. Christian Wells, Associate Professor
Department of Anthropology
University of South Florida
4202 E. Fowler Avenue, SOC 107
Tampa, FL 33620

Dr. Wells and Dr. Kimmerle:

I am in receipt of your July 8, 2013 letter seeking clarification of the Bureau of Archeological Research's (BAR) June 14, 2013 request for information regarding the University of South Florida's (USF) request for a 1A-32 archeological research permit for the excavation of human remains at the Boot Hill Cemetery at the former Arthur G. Dozier School.

I understand the importance of telling the story of the Dozier School and recognize that the significance is all the more poignant for those whose loved ones may be laid to rest on the school grounds. The Department of State has had the opportunity to assist in the effort to piece together the untold portions of the complicated history of this Florida institution. BAR issued permit numbers 1112.032 and 1213.018 to USF to facilitate efforts to identify and protect human burials. Surface-level research was authorized to determine the location of the grave sites in order to preserve the cemetery "as a valuable historical resource for Florida and surviving family members." Your work under those permits is not yet complete, and the BAR has granted USF extensions on those permits in order to continue that important work. The Department of State will continue providing assistance consistent with our authority and capability in that endeavor.

Your inquiry diverged from its original objectives when you sought a third permit with the purpose of actually exhuming the bodies from their grave sites. The Department of State does not have the statutory authority to fulfill your request. The BAR's existing statutory authority to grant archaeological research permits is restricted to the recovery of objects of historical or archeological value, not human remains, absent a danger to the grave site that actually threatens the loss or damage of those remains. Under Florida law, human bodies are not objects to be dug up for research purposes. To the contrary, the law presumes that buried human remains will rest undisturbed, and allows their intentional disinterment only in narrowly defined circumstances for which specific procedures are provided in law.

If there is reason to believe that crimes were committed at Dozier School, I share the deep concern that the truth be discovered. To be sure, your continued interaction with the Attorney General, the State Attorney, and the Medical Examiner will advance this shared goal. This agency, however, does not have any authority with respect to criminal investigations.

Your July 8, 2013 letter requested some clarification from BAR, indicating that without it you will be unable to provide all of the information requested in its June 14, 2013 letter. Because the Division does not have the authority to issue archaeological permits to excavate human remains under these circumstances, this agency is unable to take any action on your permit request.

The Department of State appreciates the efforts of the University of South Florida to identify historical resources in order to preserve and protect them for the families of the deceased and future generations, and we look forward to continuing our participation in that endeavor.

Sincerely,

Ken Detzner
Florida Secretary of State

Appendix Six

"The Tampa Atrocities"
January 30, 2014
An online commentary.

The Tampa Atrocities: Officially-sanctioned beatings, torture and death in Hillsborough County, Florida.

By Dale Cox

This is a story that the *Tampa Bay Times* would not not tell.

There is a place in Florida where beatings of jail inmates was commonplace. It is a place where those in custody were stretched out face down in public view and lashed with a leather whip for minor offenses. It is a place where the officials called upon to investigate the practice voted instead to legally authorize it. And it happened during the 20th century.

Marianna and Dozier School? Some other sleepy small town nestled in the pines and steeped in Old South tradition? No, that place is Tampa and Hillsborough County, home to the University of South Florida and the *Tampa Bay Times*.

The use of the lash by authorities in Tampa and Hillsborough County was widespread and accepted deep into the 20th century. It continued for decades and no prisoner was immune to the threat of flogging on the whim of city and county officials. Judges even beat children in the courtrooms of the city.

The *Tampa Tribune* reported in 1909 that the practice of flogging prisoners had been initiated there ten years earlier by Judge Whitaker of the municipal court. He "set a precedent," the historical account noted, "by personally applying the lash to two boy offenders convicted in his court."

The word "precedent" according to *Merriam-Webster* means "something done or said that can be used as an example or rule to be followed in the future." When Judge Whitaker beat two children in Tampa's municipal court, he set an "example or rule to be followed in the future." Hillsborough County was not shy in following that example.

On April 10, 1921, for example, the *Tampa Tribune* reported that it had received a letter from a "well-known woman resident of Clearwater" who alleged that she had witnessed the "brutal flogging of a convict."

The unidentified eyewitness said that she and several others were traveling by car between Oldsmar and Tampa on the afternoon of Thursday, April 7, when she witnessed "the most brutal act I have ever seen." In a letter to the editor of the Tribune, she described seeing a county road camp prisoner face-down on the ground beside the road as a guard beat him "with all his might with a leather strap." The sound of the beating was so loud that the witnesses could hear each of the blows as they struck the man.

The woman was unable to say how long the beating went on, but she said that it continued for the entire time she and others in the car were within sight of the road crew. She also said that it caused her to wonder what else happened in the county prison camp "where there was no public to look on."

The eyewitness raised a good question. If a guard was so bold as to force an inmate to stretch out face down by a public road for a beating that continued for an untold length of time, what else could have been taking place in Hillsborough County away from the eyes of the public? Could inmates of the county's prison camp have been maimed or even killed by the floggings they received?

The incident took place in the County Commission district of John T. Gunn, who told the Tribune that he had no reports of "extreme conduct on the part of the guards." He promised to make a "thorough investigation" of the allegations.

True to his word, Gunn did investigate. In fact, he was so impressed with the details of the beating that he recommended the implementation of flogging as a standard punishment in Hillsborough County. In fact, the Hillsborough County Commission called the county's sheriff on the carpet before a meeting of the board to demand he explain why 15 federal prisoners housed at the county jail were not turned over to the county to be used as forced laborers on its roads. The sheriff had previously told Commissioner Gunn that he was willing to allow the county to use the prisoners, but that they could not be flogged. Before the commissioners on that day in 1921, however, he changed his mind and "withdrew his restrictions."

On April 14, 1921, the *Tampa Tribune* ran letters from readers both supporting and opposing the beating of county inmates with whips. On the same day the newspaper reported that Superintendent McIntosh, who managed the work camp, had given assurances that "no color discrimination" was being made in selecting inmates for flogging. McIntosh proudly described the whipping of three men in one day, two of them white and one black. The road camp "boss" told the newspaper that floggings also took place in the state convict camp in Hillsborough County as well.

The county's investigation of the beatings at its road camp ended with a commission vote giving full sanction to flogging as a suitable punishment for inmates.

Flogging, in fact, became so popular in the Tampa Bay area that it soon spread to St. Petersburg. In 1931, ten years after Hillsborough County officially adopted flogging, a civilian group in neighboring Pinellas County started a "flogging for hire" organization. For the right amount of money, they would arrange the flogging of anyone you wanted flogged.

The commercial floggers, however, went afoul of the law when they flogged... the law. On March 8, 1931, the group kidnapped and flogged Constable F.A. Howard of Ballast Point. Arrests followed.

Despite such evidence that flogging was reaching out of control proportions around Tampa Bay, the practice continued. On November 30, 1935, officers of the Tampa Police Department seized three Union labor organizers without a warrant and carried them to police headquarters. The men were illegally questioned about their political and organizing activities as a "mob" gathered outside. When the three Socialist Party members – Joseph Shoemaker, E.F. Pulnot and S.D. Rogers – were released, they were seized on the grounds of the Tampa Police Department by the "ruffian band" that lay in wait. Carried to a remote area, they were flogged and then scalding hot tar and feathers were poured on their bodies.

Pulnot and Rogers survived the barbarous treatment, but Shoemaker did not. He died one week later from hideous injuries. Rev. G.F. Snyder of St. Paul's Lutheran Church in Tampa boldly spoke out against the atrocity, aiming his finger at "the very citadel of justice and law administration." A mass meeting was held, but public officials did not attend.

The focus of the nation fixed itself on Tampa. Florida Governor Dave Sholtz demanded a thorough investigation and labor leader Norman Thomas accused law enforcement of mishandling the investigation to "save the face of Tampa police and higher-ups." The president of the American Federation of Labor (AFL) threatened to cancel his group's planned national convention, set for Tampa in 1936.

Then came the bombshell. Six Tampa policemen were arrested on the night of December 18, 1935, on charges that they were members of the so-called "ruffian band." Shoemaker's death, it was alleged, did not result from an attack by a mob, but instead was an execution carried out with a lash and hot tar by Tampa police. A member of the city's fire department also was arrested.

A second bombshell came on January 23, 1936, when Tampa Police Chief R.G. Tittsworth was indicted by a special grand jury as an accessory to the crime. In the end, a total of 10 arrests were made in connection with the incident and Governor Sholtz appointed a special prosecutor to handle the case, saying in the process that he meant no disrespect to the Hillsborough County Solicitor, C.Jay Hardee.

The police officers were acquitted. The family of Joseph Shoemaker never received justice. There was no closure.

A national civil rights publication called it a "Whitewash" and alleged that the police officers were members of the Ku Klux Klan (KKK). Whether they were or not is impossible to prove, but the Tampa Bay area is still infested with hate groups. According to the Southern Poverty Law Center (SPLC) in Montgomery, Alabama, there are 9 hate groups active in the Tampa Bay area. These include the New Black Panther Party, Neo-Nazis, Christian Identity and the racist Skinhead group Confederate Hammerskins. By comparison, Miami and North Miami are home to three hate groups, only one-third as many as Tampa Bay. Marianna and Jackson County, home to the former Dozier School, have none.

The *Tampa Bay* Times has run story after story on the allegations of murders at Dozier School, even though 52 of the 55 people exhumed from the Dozier Cemetery are believed to have been buried there more than 75 years ago. How many stories has it published in the last two years about the officially-sanctioned beatings and death in Hillsborough County from the same exact same era? None.

I told Ben Montgomery, a reporter with the *Tampa Bay Times*, about the Tampa floggings in April 2013 and he told me he had never heard of them. I encouraged him to look into them. His paper continues to ignore the horrors that took place in Tampa even while "seeking the truth" about Marianna. Montgomery did not respond to an email asking why he elected not to report on events that took place in his own community.

Think the official violence against prisoners in the Tampa Bay area ended long before the days of the "White House Boys" at Dozier School in Marianna? Think again. In May 2012 a Pinellas County deputy was caught on video grabbing a handcuffed and seated prisoner by the throat with both hands and throwing him from his chair onto the floor. The officer was later fired.

And then in 2014 video surfaced online of a handcuffed homeless woman being pulled from a car onto the ground and then dragged across parking lot pavement by a Tampa police officer.

So far as is known no Tampa area media outlet has tried to find either the survivors of beatings or the families of individuals who were abused by authorities in Hillsborough County and the Tampa Bay area during the early 20th century. They continue, however, to run interviews and stories about alleged events that took place in Jackson County at exactly the same time in history.

The University of South Florida, meanwhile, is spending more than $600,000 of taxpayer money in a "humanitarian effort" to identify 55 unknown graves at Dozier School. How much money has USF spent to identify the 187 unknown graves at Woodlawn Cemetery within 15 minutes of the doors of its Anthropology Department?

How much money has the university spent to learn whether any beaten and abused inmates disappeared from the Hillsborough County Road Camp in the 1920s and 30s?

How much money has USF spent looking for a "lost" cemetery associated with the atrocities suffered by adults and children in Hillsborough County?

How many times has Attorney General Pam Bondi commented on the documented atrocities that took place in Tampa and Hillsborough County? How often has she called for closure for the families of the victims?

Officers from the Hillsborough County Sheriff's Department spent time in Marianna assisting USF in its exhumation of the graves from the Dozier School Cemetery. How much time did they spend last year looking into the skeletons of their own past?

I think you already know the answers to these questions.

Appendix Seven

Documented deaths at Dozier School for Boys
(Previously the Florida Reform School and Florida Industrial School for Boys)

Name	Date	Cause of Death	Burial Location
Unknown	Pre-1906	Unknown	Unknown
Unknown	Pre-1906	Unknown	Unknown
Burrell T. Morgan*	6/3/1910	Heart	Marianna
Unknown	1911	Unknown	Unknown
Bennett Evans*	11/18/1914	Fire	School Cemetery
Charles Evans*	11/18/1914	Fire	School Cemetery
Joe Wethersbee	11/18/1914	Fire	School Cemetery
Walter Fisher	11/18/1914	Fire	School Cemetery
Louis Fernandez	11/18/1914	Fire	School Cemetery
Harry Wells	11/18/1914	Fire	School Cemetery
Clifford Jefford	11/18/1914	Fire	School Cemetery
Waldo Drew**	11/18/1914	Fire	School Cemetery
Scott Martin	1915	Unknown	Unknown
Granville Rogers	1915	Unknown	Unknown
Willie Fisher	1915	Unknown	Unknown
Sim Williams	2/28/1916	Unknown	Unknown
Tillman Mohind	5/25/1916	Unknown	Unknown
James Joshua	1916	Unknown	Unknown
Thomas Aikins	4/16/1918	Unknown	Unknown
Lee Gaalsby	10/6/1918	Unknown	Unknown
George Grissam	10/23/1918	Chronic Gastritis	School Cemetery
Wilbur Smith	1918	Influenza	School Cemetery
Willie Adkins	1918	Influenza	School Cemetery
Lloyd Dutton	1918	Influenza	School Cemetery
Ralph Whiddon	1918	Influenza	School Cemetery
Hilton Finley	1918	Influenza	School Cemetery

Puner Warner	1918	Influenza	School Cemetery
Unknown	1918	Influenza	School Cemetery
Unknown	1918	Influenza	School Cemetery
Unknown	1918	Influenza	School Cemetery
Unknown	1918	Influenza	School Cemetery
Unknown	1918	Influenza	School Cemetery
Unknown*	1918	Influenza	School Cemetery?
Joseph Anderson	1919	Unknown	Unknown
Henry Murphy	1920	Died Home	Off Campus
Leonard Simmons	5/9/1919	Unknown	School Cemetery
Nathaniel Sawyer	12/12/1920	Unknown	School Cemetery
Alton Long	1920	Pneumonia	Off Campus
Wallace Ward	1921	Pneumonia	Walton Co.
Guy Hudson	8/14/1921	Drowning	Milton, FL
Arthur Williams	2/26/1921	Unknown	School Cemetery
John H. Williams	7/9/1921	Accident	School Cemetery
Samuel Morgan***	Fall 1921	Illness	School Cemetery
Schley Hunter	4/15/1922	Pneumonia	School Cemetery
Calvin Williams	12/31/1922	Unknown	School Cemetery
George Chancey, Jr.	1923	Malaria	School Cemetery
Clifford Miller	1924	Unknown	School Cemetery
Charles F. Overstreet	8/19/1924	Surgery	School Cemetery
Edward Fonders	5/18/1925	Drowning	School Cemetery
Thomas Curry	12/11/1925	Fell from Trestle	Unknown
Walter Askew	12/18/1925	Unknown	School Cemetery
Willie Sherman	1926	Unknown	Off Campus
George Johnson	1926	Unknown	Off Campus
Daniel Nollie Davis	2/8/1926	Pneumonia	School Cemetery
Earnest Mobley	1927	Unknown	Off Campus
Moses Roberts	1928	Unknown	Off Campus
Robert B. Rhoden	5/8/1929	Pneumonia	School Cemetery
Samuel Bethel	10/15/1929	Tuberculosis	School Cemetery
James C. Ansley	10/19/1929	Hazing/Burns	Marion Co.
Lee Smith	1/5/1932	Mule Accident	School Cemetery
Lonnie Frank Harrell	2/11/1932	Surgery	Hillsborough Co.
Joe Stephens	5/9/1932	Influenza	School Cemetery
James Brinson	1932	Influenza	School Cemetery
Willie Heading	1932	Influenza	School Cemetery

Sam M. Nipper	1932	Influenza	School Cemetery
Jesse D. Denson	1932	Influenza	School Cemetery
Fred Sams	1932	Influenza	School Cemetery
Lee Underwood	1932	Influenza	School Cemetery
Dary Pender	1932	Influenza	School Cemetery
Archie Shaw	1932	Influenza	School Cemetery
Oscar Elvis Murphy	1932	Struck by car	Hardee Co.
Thomas Varnadoe	10/26/1934	Pneumonia	School Cemetery
Joshua Backey	1935	Blood Poison	School Cemetery
Richard Nelson	2/23/1935	Pneumonia	School Cemetery
Robert Cato	2/25/1935	Pneumonia	School Cemetery
Grady Huff	3/5/1935	Acute Nephritis	School Cemetery
James Hammond	5/2/1936	Tuberculosis	Unknown
Robert Stephens	7/15/1937	Murdered	School Cemetery?
George Owen Smith	1940	Unknown	School Cemetery
Earl Wilson	8/31/1944	Murdered	School Cemetery
Eddie Black	5/1949	Murdered	Santa Rosa Co.
Billey Jackson	10/7/1952	Kidney Infection	School Cemetery
Clarence Cunningham	1954	Metastasis	Off Campus
George Fordom, Jr.	1/1957	Sarcoma	Off Campus
Robert J. Hewett	4/4/1960	Gunshot wound	Off Campus
Edgar Elton	7/10/1961	Heart	Lake Co.
Raymond Phillips	9/15/1961	Shot by Deputy	Alachua Co.
James Lee Fredere	6/10/1965	Auto Accident	Bladen Co., NC
Alphonso Glover	8/13/1966	Drowned	Off Campus
Martin Williams	4/28/1973	Drowned	Off Campus

*Employee
**Body not found
***No longer a student

Index

157

Books by Dale Cox

Available in Print & Kindle editions.

Milly Francis: The Life & Times of the Creek Pocahontas
The remarkable story of an American Indian woman. She survived three wars and the Trail of Tears.

The Scott Massacre of 1817
The history of the first U.S. defeat of the Seminole Wars, a battle on the Apalachicola River that led to Florida becoming part of the United States.

The Claude Neal Lynching
The ground-breaking true account of the 1934 murders of Lola Cannady and Claude Neal in Northwest Florida.

The Battle of Marianna, Florida
A detailed history of the 1864 Civil War battle that culminated the deepest penetration of Florida by Union troops during the entire war.

The Battle of Natural Bridge, Florida
A history of the battle that saved Tallahassee from capture and preserved its status as the only Southern capital city east of the Mississippi not taken by Union forces during the Civil War.

The Battle of Massard Prairie, Arkansas
An account of the 1864 Confederate attacks on Fort Smith, Arkansas, this is the only book-length treatment of these little known actions that opened the door for the greatest supply seizure of the Civil War.

Old Parramore: The History of a Florida Ghost Town
A look back through time at the fascinating rise, life and disappearance of a riverboat town on the forgotten Florida section of the famed Chattahoochee River.

Two Egg, Florida: A Collection of Ghost Stories, Legends & Unusual Facts
The stories behind the stories of some of Northwest Florida's must unique legends, including the true history of the quaint little community of Two Egg.

The Early History of Gadsden County
A fascinating look at a series of key episodes from the pre-1865 history of Gadsden County, Florida.

The History of Jackson County, Florida: The Early Years
(Volume One)
A look at the pre-Civil War history of Jackson County, focusing on Spanish missions, Native American history, the Seminole Wars, the Antebellum era and more.

The History of Jackson County, Florida: The Civil War Years*
(Volume Two)
The most detailed account ever written of a Florida county's experience during the four years of the Civil War. Details battles, raids, outlaw gangs and more.

*Also subtitled The War Between the States.

A Christmas in Two Egg, Florida
A short novel or redemption set in the quaint Northwest Florida community of Two Egg.

All books by Dale Cox are available at:

www.exploresouthernhistory.com